DATE		

Rejuvenate!

(IT'S NEVER TOO LATE)

EARTHA KITT

with
Tonya Bolden

A LISA DREW BOOK

SCRIBNER

NEW YORK LONDON TORONTO SYDNEY SINGAPORE

SCRIBNER
1230 Avenue of the Americas
New York, NY 10020

SCRIBNER and design are trademarks of Macmillan Library
Reference USA, Inc., used under license by Simon & Schuster,
the publisher of this work.

Designed by Colin Joh
Set in Schneidler

Manufactured in the United States of America

1 3 5 7 9 10 8 6 4 2

Library of Congress Cataloging-in-Publication Data
Kitt, Eartha.
Rejuvenate!: it's never too late/Eartha Kitt; with Tonya Bolden.
p. cm.
1. Aging—Psychological aspects. 2. Self-actualization (Psychology) in
middle age. 3. Self-actualization (Psychology) in old age.
4. Kitt, Eartha. I. Bolden, Tonya. II. Title.
BF724.55.A35 K57 2001
782.42164'092—dc21
[B]   00-052633

ISBN 0-7432-0224-4

To Kitt, Jason, and Rachel:
Thank you for helping me stay balanced.

To my fans and friends, who have allowed me
to stay on my path.

Contents

Rejuvenate!

Warm Up

When the year 2000 commenced, I was seventy-two years old and had quite a lot on my plate. I played to sold-out crowds at Manhattan's Café Carlyle through mid-February (two shows a night, six days a week). Rehearsals for *The Wild Party* began in January (six days a week—long hours), with the show in previews in March and fully up and running in mid-April (six evenings a week plus Wednesday and Saturday matinees). I also had the goal of completing this book by May Day, 2000. In between, there were out-of-town appearances—here a day in Charleston, South Carolina, there a day in Savannah, Georgia, et cetera, et cetera.

"The gods are good," I thought as I sat in my room at the Carlyle Hotel, getting ready for my very last performance of 1999.

Indeed, the gods had been more than good, considering my beginnings: ugly duckling Eartha Mae, born out of wedlock and into poverty on a cotton plantation in South Carolina, then given away because Mama's husband-to-be said he didn't want "that yella gal" in his house. The people she was given to—were they close or distant relatives? She never knew. Of one thing there was no doubt. These people were cruel: beating Eartha Mae, poorly feeding Eartha Mae, working her like a dog.

And when this Thursday's child was brought up North, to Harlem, and found a new mama in an aunt, there were no great expectations for her. Factory worker or domestic worker—surely this would be her lot. Instead, there were rescues for her and her irrepressible love of words, of song, of the dance.

The world of possibilities began to open when she was accepted into the School of Performing Arts. Life widened a few years later when she became a member of the Katherine Dunham Dance Troupe. Before she was twenty years old, shy little Eartha Mae had performed with the Dunham dancers in America, Mexico, England, Paris, and elsewhere in Europe.

Then came her debut as a cabaret performer in Paris in 1949, which led to countless engagements at some of the poshest clubs in Europe, at one of which Orson Welles found her and cast her as Helen of Troy in his interpretation of *Faust,* which became a part of the show *An Evening with Orson Welles.*

It was when I asked, "Why me?" that Orson said, "You are the most exciting woman in the world." Many people have thought that this statement pertained to my sex appeal. But there was more. "You are the most exciting woman in the world" was not the whole of Orson's response. After that, he said this: "You represent all women of all ages. You have no place or time."

What an affirmation. As a youngster, I had struggled so with feelings of not belonging, of not being wanted, of not fitting in anywhere. Yet, I found that to survive I had to learn to adapt to anywhere, and I had always felt that I had to accept being different.

"Who is the real you?" someone once asked me.

"The me who happens to be in front of you at the moment, that's the real me."

The more I surrendered to myself, to the self that would not be limited and narrowly defined, the more glorious a time I had with *me* and with life. I stayed open, ready, breathless even, for adventure: eager to go wherever my talents might take me.

So, yes, I went with *An Evening with Orson Welles* around Europe in 1950, and then through other doors that opened, including New York's Village Vanguard, from where I went on to a twenty-five-week run at the Blue Angel. It was there that producer Leonard Sillman saw me and snapped me up for Broadway: for his *New Faces of 1952.* Quickly, the whole town was talking about me, especially about my "Bal Petit Bal" and "Monotonous," which were showstoppers for a year. Then came the *New Faces* national tour and the film, which led to more engagements—and Eartha Kitt had become a bona fide star.

Eartha Mae was awed by how far and widely she had traveled. She was stunned and grateful that the public had adopted Eartha Kitt and made Eartha Mae feel worthwhile. Never presuming, but always hopeful, she looked forward to the rest of the journey, which did, in fact, continue—rich, diverse, and intensely rewarding: best-selling records; more work in the theater (a Tony nomination in 1954 for my role in *Mrs. Patterson* was definitely a high point); work in films (including *St. Louis Blues* and *Anna Lucasta*); more nightclub engagements (from the Plaza Hotel's Persian Room to the Talk of the Town in London); more concerts around the world with the pleasure of singing in more than ten languages. There was television, too (the *Omnibus* presentation of

Salome; I Spy, for which I received an Emmy nomination; *Mission Impossible*—and, yes, joining the cast of *Batman* as Catwoman was purrrr-fect for me!).

And in the mid-1950s, I had been celebrated with a star on Hollywood Boulevard's Walk of Fame. Could it get any better than this?

There was a time when many people did not think so. The buzz was that my career was kaput after I spoke out against the Vietnam War, incurring the government's wrath. But Eartha Mae survived that (through Eartha Kitt). Just as she had survived the gossip about her being a sex-crazed creature. Just as she had survived great loves lost (millionaire John Barry Ryan III, cinema-house scion Arthur Loew Jr., and founder of Revlon, Charles Revson). Just as she had survived a marriage to Bill McDonald that did not last, but which did produce the greatest delight of her life, her daughter, Kitt.

Onward, forward, upward. How? By staying ready— mind, body, and soul. Ready for the club owners and fans in Europe who cherished me when work was hard to come by in America, and ready to get work in America when the "climate" changed.

From the 1970s onward I have been productive, because I

kept myself ready: ready for more recordings, more concerts and nightclub engagements (at home and abroad), for *Timbuktu!* and another Tony nomination, for more parts in films as different as *Boomerang* and *Harriet the Spy;* ready to be The Wicked Witch in the national tour of *The Wizard of Oz;* ready for *The Wild Party;* and, yes, ready on December 31, 1999, for my umpteenth performance at Café Carlyle, where I had been engaged every winter since the late 1980s.

It was one o'clock in the morning of January 1, 2000, when I bid the second audience adieu. I went to bed supremely appreciative for being alive—truly alive, with Kitt and her children in an adjoining suite—alive to greet the new year, the new decade, the new century, the new millennium (depending on your math). I was grateful, too, for a long life without any devastating illness. To still be here and to still be doing, doing, doing—how fantastic!

"Don't you ever get tired?" people asked when I was sixty, sixty-five, seventy, and when I turned seventy-three in mid-January 2000.

Only the young get tired—the young, and the elders who have given up on themselves, who think there's nothing more for them but to wait for the gods to call.

Life is too marvelous, too wonderful, too brimming with adventures for me to get tired. After a performance, I may feel spent but not tired, and in no way weary. I know this feeling of exhaustion. It is always a sign for me to refuel, to rejuvenate.

My formula is simple: foods that are right for me (at the right time, in the right amounts) plus continual exercise of the mind and the body.

Some who know me only from afar may think that the body has always been my first priority. *Au contraire.* I love the brain no less than I love the body. (Perhaps more, if the truth be told.) When the two are functioning well in concert, there is nothing in the world more exciting. So I strive to make the body love the mind, and the mind love the body, keeping the spirit vigorous as a consequence. This, I feel, is the key to my unfeeble longevity: more than twenty-five thousand days on this earth and no complaints. There's the occasional bronchial brouhaha, the legacy of a terrible case of whooping cough I had when my Southern lungs made first contact with New York's winter air. Owing to a bit of arthritis, my joints aren't always jumping. Still, I say, no complaints. What ailments I have are nothing in light of the quality of my quantity of years. (Keep moving! Don't let the limbs catch up with the years!)

I may be genetically predisposed to longevity, but I will never know for sure. Neither my mama in South Carolina nor my mama in Harlem lived to be my age. As for my father, I never had a clue. The mystery of my origins meant that I could never gamble on any advantage of genes when it came to having a healthy mind and body.

Certainly, my calling as a dancer, singer, and actress gave me incentive to take care of myself; however, behind all that discipline of proper diet and exercise was a zeal for life: to live to the fullest in every aspect of my existence. Because I have, when I turned fifty, sixty, seventy, I didn't look "my age," I didn't move "my age," I didn't feel "my age."

And it's never too late. Hence, this book in which I share the fundamental ways of being, thinking, and doing that have kept me productive, content, whole, and free of fear about "getting old."

I have never yearned to stay young in the common sense, but rather to stay me: the me committed to embracing her uniqueness; the me who feels no shame in championing and cherishing herself; the me who accepts aging as a natural process (not a disease!) and who is saying to the gods, "Thank you, thank you," when I take care of me.

I encourage you, darling reader, no matter what your age, to make a commitment to take care of yourself. (If you have already made this commitment—keep it up!) We are living longer, you know. You owe it to yourself and to your loved ones to do all that you can to increase the possibility that the quality of your days is as good as it can get if you are granted twenty thousand days, thirty thousand days, or perhaps a century.

May the exercises in this book help you make the most of each day, the most of yourself—to keep the desire to be self-sufficient, to love thyself, and to keep moving.

Eartha

ONE

Breathe

Breathe in through the nose, pushing the breath as far as you can into the lower regions of the body.

For as long as you can, hold . . . hold . . . hold. . . . Slowly, exhale through the mouth until your stomach is completely deflated. Repeat twice (or as many times as you can). Take time out throughout your day for some deep breathing. (Let it be your coffee break.)

When we breathe thoroughly, we allow the organs their fulfillment of oxygen, which needs to go all through the body to give it strength, to bring up poisons, toxins—to cleanse (and burn off a bit of fat in the process). According to Asian sages, one deep breath is worth ten minutes of our lives. Habitual quality breathing can also help keep the stomach flat and the back strong.

I take in life. I choose life. I embrace the reality that life is a cycle.

Just as shallow breathing is not good enough for the body and mind, so shallow relationships to experiences are injurious to our health. Whatever the matter—fair, foul, grim, glorious—I breathe it in, knowing that whatever needs to be expelled will be.

Were I not committed to "inhaling" and "exhaling" experiences, I might not have survived the disappointments I have known over the years, especially in my fifty-plus years in show business. I also would not have learned to sing with truth and verve such songs as "I'm Still Here" had I not been able to breathe through so many rejections.

In the early days, from casting directors, I got—

"You don't fit in."

"You're not like anybody we know."

"You don't look like something we're used to."

From the recording companies—

"Your voice is too weird, strange."

On down through the years, along with successes, I have had many sorrows to breathe through, such as not getting the part of The Witch in Stephen Sondheim's *Into the Woods*.

It was to be a temporary job, a six-week engagement to replace Bernadette Peters. I was absolutely elated over the chance, because *Into the Woods* was such a wonderful, such an intelligent, such a beautiful creation, and The Witch was a stellar character.

At the audition, I had the finest time with my prepared reading of the material I had been sent. After the initial audition, Sondheim sprung a rap song on me. "Now try this," he said.

I rippled through the song without a hitch.

"Oh! I didn't know that you knew how to speak so clippingly on the tongue."

"Well, I did study Shakespeare."

We all laughed and we all shook hands. My audition, I thought, was stupendous—and that is what I was told. Accolades overflowed. "You've got the part!" seemed on the tips of their tongues.

Though I have never been one to count the chickens prematurely, I leapt, I romped, I jumped for joy when I returned home.

Playing The Witch would allow me to use *all* of myself: my athletic self (Witch climbing the ropes), my naughty self (Witch being mean to the daughter), my comedic self (Witch so witty), my self who would be ecstatic to be once again on Broadway!

"Oh, God, please, let me have this part!"

I didn't get it.

It was as though I had been deflated. My whole heart and soul was deflated.

I did much walking that weekend, near my home, with my dog, July. Walking . . . walking . . . walking around and through the woods—not missing the irony.

I walked familiar paths, seeing things as if for the first time. Same skyline, same hills, same trees, but it was all so different— shapes, colors, scents. I became so sensitive to everything, particularly to the gods' power to give and to take away, to form and re-form.

It was as if every hurt I had ever known since the day I was given away in the South had just occurred; and I knew I had to not stop the opening up. I let myself open up even more, heart-wise, soul-wise.

So sensitive and . . . so much more appreciative I became. Now that something had been denied me, I was acutely aware of how much else there was to share and to become a part of.

"You didn't get it, Eartha," whispered that abandoned, abused South Carolina girl. "They don't want you."

I wrestled with why-why-why.

The fans, the critics—they say that I am so good at my craft, that I am one of the best. I am told that there is nobody like me, that I am unique, wonderful, beautiful, intelligent— *Why didn't I get this part for which I was so fabulously made?*

"You didn't get it, Eartha. They don't want you."

I wept a lot that weekend, surrendering to the cleansing to be had through tears, and self-analysis. The hurts from childhood, the hurts that *never* leave, but leave a scar on the tissues of the soul. They wait there. Open wounds again that some incident salts.

There I was up in my sixties. Not a newcomer, not an ingenue on tiptoe for that first break. The first or the five hundredth—it was all the same. I had been *so* passionate about playing The Witch. I would have been untrue to myself had I tried to be stoic about the loss. I *had* to mourn, to grieve, to wash away my grief with groaning, crying, sighing. With it all, I did a lot of deep, deep breathing. I filled myself to capacity with the sylvan air. I exhaled thoroughly. Oxygen. Oxygen. Oxygen.

"Open the window," a doctor often advises. No matter if it is chilly outside, there are times when we need to open a window and take in new, renewing air, no matter what the climate.

So it is with our souls. When we open ourselves to a situation we revitalize our minds, our spirits, absolving the hurt and thus becoming able to use it in a positive way.

Most definitely, I champion the tears. How sad it is that as we "mature," the less some of us cry.

It's not appropriate, they say.

It's not respectable, they say.

It's not—blah, blah, blah, blah, blah.

Why, then, do we have tears? If only babies are to cry, why do our tears not disappear when we "come of age"? A mother's milk, when no longer needed, dries up.

Nothing in Creation is for nothing. Nature has a way of getting rid of what she knows is making us uncomfortable. When a speck of whatever flies into your eye, if the eye is functioning properly, you will involuntarily blink as water rises sufficiently to flush away that bit of grit.

My crying over not getting the part in *Into the Woods* was critical to my ability to release the hurt and sadness. Had I not inhaled and exhaled *Into the Woods,* I might have become a real witch, forgetting to keep my soul clean and ready for something wonderful.

What a pity to strive to be so emotionally streamlined to the point of stripping oneself of mourning time, whether the loss is a love, a job, or even an argument. True mourning time is vital, something the ancients all over the world understood so well, and therefore, they gave thought and time to elaborate mourning rituals.

"Get over it!" That oh-so-postmodern dictum can be perilous. Do we ever really get over a loss? Certainly, we can overcome and move beyond. But get over it?

A sorrow ceases to be a stumbling block when we breathe through the experience, when we go to the source, to the why of the grieving.

"No, you didn't get the part, Eartha."

"Eartha Mae, now, how many times in your life have you had disappointments that you know you've had to grieve away, talk away, walk through? And how many times have you found rescue in the thought that something wonderful will happen?"

"Something wonderful will happen?"

"Yes, Eartha Mae, something wonderful will happen. The gods have not let us down thus far. We must stay on the alert for the gods' next handout."

"But you didn't get it, Eartha. They don't want—"

When I learned that I was not cast as The Witch because they wanted a television personality, I was greatly relieved of the pain. I was about 90 percent better at that point. It wasn't that they didn't want *me*. It wasn't personal. The truth, they say, will set you free. Soon, I was me again.

I went about doing lots of what-nots that needed attending to. I answered fan mail. I mended things: a hole in a settee, a tear in a piece of clothing. I also prepared myself for an engagement in Los Angeles.

There, in my performances, I drew upon the recent rejection, injecting the hurt into my songs, sad and funny ones alike. Once again, I was reminded that nothing is good-for-nothing.

It was while I was in Los Angeles that Cameron Mackintosh came to see me, offering me a role: to replace the actress playing Carlotta, the "I'm Still Here" girl, in his production of James Goldman and Stephen Sondheim's *Follies,* which was running in London.

Having inhaled and exhaled that *Into the Woods* loss, I was in fantastic shape to breathe in deeply this *c'est si bon,* brand-new opportunity. London and Sondheim—two of my favorite things!

Something wonderful will happen.

I dare say we sometimes have as much trouble taking in

terrifically wonderful happenings. Is this not another kind of holding of the breath, of shallow breathing?

Do you find yourself holding back on tears of joy, on rich laughter, full hugs, broad smiles? Why? Have you been listening to what "they" say? Not mature? Not proper?

This is your life! Take it in!

Sometimes, at a child's antics or a really funny joke, I laugh myself to tears, and I love it! I love to laugh heartily, to give vent to delight, without fretting about "acting my age."

Breathing room. How dearly we need that. I think we do ourselves a disservice when we insist on reserving breathing room for the weekend, or the calendared vacation. I am forever seizing chances for breathing room in my every day.

Drive time is often breathing time for me. When engaged at Café Carlyle, I have used the drive to and from Manhattan and my home in Westchester to process the performance I hope for or the one just given. During other drives, I process other experiences, decisions, and dilemmas. (Usually, as I am thinking, I am also doing some isometrics, such as squeezing the buttocks or doing tummy tucks or breathing deeply.)

During this breathing time, I might also marvel at life all

around me (as much as I can see). I behold the colors of a season. I take note of the changing surroundings as I move from much sun to less sun (or vice versa), as I move from lots of steel and concrete to skylines dominated by nature's constructions. I think about how much I love living among an abundance of trees (all the better for breathing).

Whenever I have journeyed somewhere for the very first time, I have always tried to rise early so that I could *feel* the place, taking in the sights, the sounds, the different air. It is a way of centering myself in the where-I-am, of becoming a part of a new environment, knowing that were I to cast myself as a mere visitor, the experience would be shallow.

Years ago, in Swaziland, while standing on the balcony of my hotel room, as I watched a gorgeous sunrise, I watched the Africans moving through the woods, across the meadow, in their native dress, and with bundles of I knew not what upon their heads. Long minutes passed without a car or a truck passing by, and suddenly I was no stranger to this place. I was seeing how similar this scene was to scenes from the South of my youth. I felt connected. That hour or so of breathing time on that hotel balcony was the foundation for the fine time I had in subsequent explorations of life in Swaziland.

How some people can get bored bewilders me. There is so much to engage us when "nothing" is going on. To see it, we need only allow ourselves room to breathe, to be. For this, one needs a healthy attitude toward solitude: to be comfortable being alone with yourself.

Alone Time. I have never feared it. In fact, I have relished it. There is nothing like some Alone Time to process problems, triumphs, hopes, to get clarity on the core you and where life beckons.

There was an interview on the *NewsHour* in 1999 with that master of pantomime, Marcel Marceau—seventy-six at the time and still performing and teaching. This interview included a discussion of one of Marceau's classic pieces, which I have seen many times: "Mask Maker," the tragicomic routine of a man moving from laughing face to crying face, until at one point he becomes trapped in the laughing face, unable to take it off.

"And in the end is revealed the solitude of man—the moment of truth, also, when man is himself left in a certain solitude," remarked Marceau. And he added, "It's not sad for me, because solitude is not sad, because it's a deep reflection about life." Further on in the interview, Marceau noted, "But it's important to go deep in the roots of ourselves, and from the silence, there's music."

The ideal time for deep reflection is when we are not drenched in noise-noise, people-people, clatter, so much chatter. There are times, however, when we need to seize breathing room in the midst of the din. The busier one's life, the more one needs to be able to enter into solitude in the midst of the madding crowd.

Often, at a cocktail party I have desperately needed breathing room. To walk away and into a corner would attract too much attention. So right where I stand or sit, I tuck into my trunk of solitude and silence and take myself in my mind on a trip. I return when someone calls my name, or perhaps someone says—

"Eartha, don't you think?"

"Beg your pardon?"

For the mind to wander is not necessarily a bad thing. Often, it is a sign that you are in need of some breathing room, a little time to yourself (because the conversation is boring).

As the years pass, some become unnerved by the possibility that they will have all too much Alone Time. The children are living far away, or perhaps they are near, but busy-busy with their lives. The spouse has passed on. Friends have passed on. Enemies, too. There are fewer and fewer people with whom you can share remembrances of things past.

This can be disturbing. However, if Alone Time is sought out, savored, and even celebrated, when the inhaling and exhaling are done, we are refreshed with insights as to what we can do to keep from being lonely—more than that, to be productive and very alive. Remember the words of Marceau: ". . . from the silence, there's music."

Listen to the tune, tap to the rhythm, let your soul dance, and you will discover what to do. Instead of "Woe is me, I'm so lonely," you might volunteer your talents to an organization. You might drop your pride and frankly let your children or grandchildren know that you would like to spend more time with them. You might take the initiative with others as well, even make new friends. Who knows what you might find yourself doing that draws people to you. Without some deep breathing, you may not get to this place. Instead, you may become a grump. Perhaps you will resort to bribing, guilting, or otherwise manipulating children, grandchildren, the neighbor's teen to spend time with you, only to discover that companionship that has been commandeered does not satisfy, and that your neediness actually repels people.

Breathing through something, engaging in some deep reflection, allows us to see the give-and-take of life. Just like physical breathing: air in, air out, stomach expands, stomach retracts. Like physical breathing, reflection clears the mind. Don't you feel better when during a tense moment, you take a deep breath and a stretch or go for a walk?

We also advance our well-being when, instead of immediately responding to an annoyance or insult, we "take a breath."

The first and last time that I struck someone was eons ago. I was about seven or eight years old, recently arrived in Harlem, where I was to live with my aunt.

One of the best things that happened to me up North was a beautiful party dress my aunt gave me. Except for an Easter dress she had sent down South (and which, after one wearing, had mysteriously disappeared), the only dresses I had ever known were sticky, itchy things made of croaker sacks. And here was this happiness of blue, red, and green in some fancy fabric, perhaps a fine-grade cotton or silk. It was the most precious thing I had ever had to call my own.

So I was beyond perturbed when I caught Joyce with my dress on. Joyce was a girl about two years older than I was, whose family my aunt and I were rooming with. And there she was one day walking down the hall in my dress without my permission.

The next thing I knew, I had Joyce down on the floor. I do not remember feeling anything, but I do remember that I was choking her. I don't think I would have murdered the girl; still, it was a good thing that her father pulled me off of her. (My dress, I am glad to say, was none the worse.)

Had I taken a breath, I would not have behaved so horribly. But, of course, I was a child, still forming.

I learned a lot from that. For one, I realized how strong I was (from cotton picking, hauling wood from the yard, slopping the hogs, and all the other labor I had been forced to do down South). And this strength could do evil. Somewhere in my becoming self, I realized the value of taking a breath.

Raw rage let loose without thought to consequence is akin to breathing merely from the chest: not good, not salutary for the soul. When we take a breath, however, we allow ourselves to respond to a situation more productively, whether that response is simply to do nothing, or to express, intelligently, our disagreement or displeasure. Unprocessed rage can seriously rend relationships, as well as age us.

Had I taken a breath, I would not have jumped Joyce. I would have told her (spoiled child that she was) that it is not nice to take what does not belong to you. I would have told her that had she asked permission to try on the dress, I would have said yes.

After this incident, Joyce treated me with greater respect, it is true. How much better it would have been, however, had she come to respect me not as a consequence of brute force.

When someone annoys or infuriates you, before you respond, take a breath. Take a deep breath.

Deep breathing is also a barricade against the low-grade bad mood that can sometimes overtake us: that out-of-sortsness spawned by something such as the weather not cooperating with your plans. The rainfall or the snowfall may not be convenient. It may even trigger a little tension. However, if you stop and breathe, you will see that the phenomenon is part of life, part of the cycle, and the tension will abate.

Take in the "bad" weather. Think about what muscles it will allow you to work—attention to detail on the road or while walking, perhaps. If we are not growling about what we cannot control, we are better able to transform what would be negative energy into positive energy.

Breathe in the rain and think about how necessary water is to life: bird life, plant life, your life. A stone changes from the falling of the rain; so do mountains. Water changes everything. I think of rain as God's tears washing away in order to enhance.

Rain, hail, snow, fog—I breathe it in—and I think, "There's a reason for this"—just as there is a reason for the sunshine that brings such delight. I do not squander my energies damning a day. I do not allow the notion of "bad" weather to trick me into a "bad" mood. I take in the is-ness of the day. When I exhale, I am better able to focus on what I need to do to journey through it. I am open for some new thing to learn or to experience. The alternative—becoming cranky and cantankerous—holds no appeal for me. (And when I am cranky, often it is a sign that I am hungry.)

The weather is a metaphor for what we cannot control; and I weather the weather by breathing.

Inhale.

Exhale.

Thanks to my habit of full, proper breathing, I am better able to handle the other "exercises" the gods would have me do.

Jot down experiences you have yet to fully breathe through and then make up for lost time (and healing, in some cases) by really processing these matters.

1. _____

2. _____

3. _____

4. _____

5. _____

6. _____

7. _____

8. _____

9. _____

10. _____

TWO

Stretch

Stand on level flooring, with your feet flat and at ease. Drop your head (chin touching chest ideally) and let your arms dangle at your sides. Pull the stomach in tight, tight, tight, tight, tight, and pull the body up.

Slowly, raise your arms above your head. Be a flower opening to the dew . . . the sun . . . a cerulean sky. Then—s-t-r-e-t-c-h! Reach for the sky for thirty seconds (or as long as you can)—and believe that you are beautiful! Then, reach one arm up at a time (ten times on each side). Repeat this entire exercise twice. Be sure to breathe thoroughly, with your stomach behaving like a balloon: when you are breathing in, the stomach should extend, and when breathing out, the stomach should deflate. As with deep breathing, stretching is the sort of exercise that is good to do at various points throughout your day—especially if you're tense.

It was 1951 and I was in Athens, Greece, with time to spare before my show at a club named Constantine's. I had decided to revive my spirit with lunch outdoors at the Acropolis. My lunch dates: Socrates and Plato.

I'd spied these thinkers during my self-education. Back in the States, in *Life* magazine, I believe, I had come across an article about some must-read books. This article listed some two dozen paramount books, claiming that if one were to devour the list, one would have the equivalent of a college education. That list became a passion, a quest.

Hungrily, expectantly, I (who'd bid adieu to formal schooling at about sixteen—I had to work) made my way through *Life*'s list of books. I had read perhaps half a dozen or so of them when on this buoyant Greek day, with a Mediterranean equivalent of a ham-and-cheese sandwich and a demi bottle of inglorious wine, I began my acquaintance with the two ancient Athenians through the *Dialogues* and *Plato's Republic*. The food was plebeian but the company, the setting—so sublime.

The reading was, so to speak, quite a stretch, and in the doing, reaching, striving—*stretching!*—there was Olympian growth. Ideas. New thoughts. New questions. Deeper thinking. A more vivacious worldview. It was a tremendous exercising of my mental muscle, and so very useful for the upcoming, perpetual reading I would do. Shakespeare, Joyce, Faulkner, Goethe, Tennessee Williams, Kahlil Gibran, Lao-tzu, *more, more, more*—without ever forsaking my love for a good mystery à la Agatha Christie. (I despair of people who devour books solely to prove that they are knowledgeable. Most definitely, there is learning to be had, but I feel that one should leave a book with more than book knowledge and the ability to quote–end quote. I have always supposed that a book's preeminent purpose is to prod me to think for myself, to come to my own conclusions, to find, refind, refine my own philosophy by which I wish to live. This is what moves many people to keep a journal on their reading, from musings to epiphanies. Not a bad idea.)

Reading is not the only way I have stretched and sharpened my mind over the years, but it has definitely been primo. And over the years I have felt that stretching the mind is as important and as necessary as stretching the body. In stretching the mind, we stretch our emotions and other aspects of the inner self, which should impact the outer self.

In this age of easy access to the world of ideas and creations, with our abundance of books, tapes, art spots, readings, schools, and open-air you-name-it, it is not arduous to stretch the mind. So why not—

Read a novel out of a culture different from yours.

Read a book of nonfiction on a subject about which you know zero.

Gaze at some art or tune in to some music with which you are not on intimate terms.

Prepare a meal you have never dared before.

Take a class in something that long ago intrigued you, but, alas, you never indulged because doing so seemed too much a whimsy, not "practical." One need not become an expert. Dabbling, in and of itself, is a wonder-worker! Should the dabbling lead to a full-fledged avocation—bravo! (Crocheting, knitting, and needlepoint have been of enormous value to me and the stretching of my mind. In an airplane or a car, in a hotel room or in my own room, through these handicrafts I have created memorials to where my time went, records of the passage of precious minutes, hours. In the process, I have also created home furnishings that contribute to the harmony between home and soul.)

Another way to stretch is to go somewhere off the beaten path. It need not be abroad. It need not be an extravaganza. This trip could be to a state across country, or up or down from you—a place where you know not a soul, a place whose rhythms will be new to you. Your destination could even be a nearby city, county—a wherever, just so long as it represents a change of venue. (I have found no place to be more beautiful or interesting than America. So I say spend "vacation" time discovering America.)

Too, there's that wonderful-terrible contraption that was once a novelty and is now a "necessity"—the television.

Boob tube or mind-expander—the choice is ours. Your mind will thank you if you tune in to the health food that is available via *Nova, Nature,* the *American Experience,* and so much else from PBS as well as from the Discovery Channel, the History Channel, Lifetime, C-SPAN, and any number of political talk shows. It is not difficult to change the channel, from the frivolous to the truly fascinating and mind-building (though we need a little of the frivolous, too).

Another principle that has served me well is that of seeking out and cultivating relationships with people who cherish the life of the mind and with whom I can engage in meaningful talk: conversations in which ideas are exchanged and riddles are pondered—with ample room for laughter. (Whatever happened to real conversation—talking *to* one another rather than *at*?)

All these years later, I still feel nourished by the fantastic exchanges I had with friends and acquaintances in the cafés of

Europe. In Paris, for example, over a grog and whatever little food we could afford at a place such as Café des Fleurs, our little gang of dancers, singers, painters, writers would enrich ourselves daily with debates and analyses of personal and world events. We talked about everything. Sometimes James Baldwin, Jean-Paul Sartre, Jean Gabin, and Jean Cocteau were among the thinkers who enhanced our conversations. (In that "age" of existentialism there were many discussions about Sartre and Kierkegaard or whatever we had read or seen.)

When my work did not bring me into natural contact with great minds, I sought them out, such as when in the 1950s I asked to meet Jawaharlal Nehru when I was in New Delhi, and Albert Einstein when I was in New York doing *Mrs. Patterson.* "All they can say is no" was how I responded to those who thought I was dreaming impossible dreams. But Nehru and Einstein did not say no.

The dinner I had with Nehru (with Lady Mountbatten present) and the morning meeting with Einstein (over tea and cake in his home in Princeton, New Jersey) definitely enhanced the way I thought about the world and my relationship to it. With Einstein (with whom I did not discuss the theory of relativity), most memorable was a comment he made as he watched me looking out the window at a flock of pigeons circling the tower of a Princeton building. "You see," he said, "every morning about eleven o'clock and every evening at four, they do their exercise. They are so disciplined; isn't it a shame that human beings are not so disciplined?"

I have never been scared to converse with minds mightier than mine because learning has been more important to me than feeling like a know-it-all in a crowd. When I felt out of my depth, I listened intently and asked questions in search of clarity. Of course, if you get hooked on conversation that enlivens and exhilarates the mind, you may find yourself unfit for chitchat, gossip, and the like. But I doubt that you will miss all that. And in nourishing your mind, you might want to reconsider whom you regard as a friend. The best friends are those who stretch you or help you stretch. Anyone who does not enhance your life is—well, let's just say that celebrities are not the only people who have hangers-on.

Undoubtedly, there are bundles of things you can do to stretch your mind, and the price of the ticket need not be dear. In fact, many things will cost you nothing.

Sometimes, when I am on the road and the traffic is dense, I concoct brain games. I might memorize license plates. I might speculate on the life of a fellow traveler—occupation, age, marital status, dreams even—based on whatever details I can see (clothing, adornment, hairstyle, posture, and the vehicle, of course). Sometimes, if I am at a stoplight, I count the number of pedestrians who cross my path before my light turns green. Half the fun is in what I can fathom while idling.

An open-eyed walk around the neighborhood—seeing, really *seeing,* your surroundings—can do wonders. Seeing provokes questioning, reasoning, wondering. Whether or not you reach resolution as to the how of birdsong or the why of a pile of refuse, your mind will be stretched.

Whatever you discover from a simple walkabout (or lookabout from a porch or terrace) need not have a practical application at the moment. If you have no place to "put" your discovery (even if it's merely a new question), that's absolutely fine, I believe: it is okay to be curious just to be curious. Nothing goes to waste: every moment is part of your being, a stitch in the knitting of life. Whatever piece of knowledge you come into, whatever bit of wonderment you allow yourself, somewhere along the line it will be of benefit to you, or to someone you love.

Sometimes a little curiosity may be your entrée into a

whole new world, as happened with one of the great loves of my life, Charlie Revson. By his own admission, once upon a time Charlie was a bum, a drunk, not much of what one would call a man. One day, he woke up in some dive of a motel not remembering how the hell he had gotten there. He looked at himself in the mirror and saw what he had become, and in him stirred a yearning to change his life.

On his way to get a cup of coffee, with just two bits in his pocket, Charlie saw a little man selling a tiny jar of cold cream for ten cents. Charlie's curiosity got the best of him, and he bought a jar. Over his five-cent cup of coffee, he got the idea of having the cold cream analyzed. He had a friend who was an amateur scientist (with a lab in his garage), and to this friend he took that jar of cold cream. With curiosity satisfied, Charlie and his friend got a loan of $300 from a bank and started the business that became Revlon.

Curiosity might not make you a millionaire, but it will definitely profit you. Curiosity is an excellent elixir. We adults do well to watch the children.

My daughter, Kitt, was such a curious one—with her steady stream of what's-thats and why-does-this and how-come-thats. Because I never quashed her curiosity, when she was one and two and three and beyond, she helped me stay in touch with the power and the splendor of curiosity. My grandchildren, Jason and Rachel, have carried on their mother's legacy: at one and two and three and beyond, their infectious curiosity has certainly kept me stretching, something I've been doing since I was a child.

Could I be more than just a "yella gal" from South Carolina? Could I not be the nothing others thought me? It was this curiosity and zest for life that gave me the courage to follow the urging of a teacher and take a test for admission into the School of Performing Arts. I was terrified; yet, I saw it through—and was admitted.

I stretched myself when a friend dared me to audition for Katherine Dunham's dance company. I had no audition outfit, no routine, no idea what to do. I saw it through and I was accepted into the company, eventually becoming a featured dancer and vocalist.

Years later, after Mexico, after a film in Hollywood, after touring with the company through England, in Paris, then on to elsewhere and back again to Paris, the owner of a nightclub,

Carroll's, invited me to have my own show. There was no guarantee of a long run at Carroll's. Moreover, from Dame Dunham there was no vote of confidence.

Do I stay with the dance company and its relative security?

Do I go solo so many thousands of miles away from home?

Being in Europe had already caused me to stretch in many ways. I'd had to learn languages; I'd had to adapt to customs (and there was also much stretching of dollars, pounds, francs, and lire).

Stay with what is familiar or stay with what was becoming familiar?

I think my soul reached back to my past, reminding me that life belongs to the limber.

Back to the test for the School of Performing Arts, to the audition for Dunham's company, and to my transplantation to New York City with its razzle-dazzle, hustle-bustle, and fascinating—but frightening—rhythms.

My first night at Carroll's was a terrific success. The engagement lasted much longer than planned. That job led to other jobs, such as the engagement at Constantine's, where on a brilliant day I stretched myself into Socrates and Plato, pausing here and there to think about what I had read. While

I thought, I did stretching exercises, as I looked out over the city, as I touched every rock (so to speak), as I breathed in the spirit of the philosophers.

I kept stretching in other ways as well. There was the time, with two months between engagements, that I took advantage of a travel plan that allowed one to visit certain main cities around the world on one ticket. That's how I first visited New Delhi, where I dared to ask to have dinner with Nehru.

There was the time my husband remarked that I was not intelligent enough to play chess. I promptly purchased a pocket-size chess game and a book on chess. I studied and practiced during the airplane ride to London for an engagement at Talk of the Town. There, I practiced some more with friends. When I returned home, I asked my husband to teach me to play chess.

I won. (It gave me great pleasure when my grandson began learning chess with that same little set I had learned on.)

What now comes to mind when you think of yourself and s-t-r-e-t-c-h? People to see? Places to visit? Books to read? Films to see? Getting clarity on King Arthur, Siddhartha, your mother? The source of the mermaid myth? The meaning of

A.D., B.C., B.C.E., quid pro quo, auto-da-fé, the ankh, and Rx¿ What exactly *is* the Federal Reserve¿ Whence the "butter" in butterfly¿

Think of all the things you have ever wondered about, pondered the meaning of. How about the many times you have asked yourself, "How did they do that¿" Go out and find out.

Above all, be curious about your body. Think about how you are put together. When I look at a skeleton in a doctor's office, I never cease to be amazed at how our bones hold us together. Looking at a diagram of the whole unit—skin, veins, toes, nails, hair, heart, kidneys, lungs—wow! I marvel at how woman is inside and how man is inside, and the difference between them.

The teeth, the tongue, the eyes, the nose—all for a purpose, all to be respected, cherished, appreciated, loved, and *taken care of.*

I believe that when you stretch the mind, the body will follow. A mind that is open to stretching is a mind that will seize opportunities for the body to stretch.

Imagine yourself at a bus stop or waiting in line at the post office or at a checkout counter. Your body could just be still, or you could use the waiting time to do toe raises, stretching the calves and the rest of the leg. (If you're the impatient sort, how much better for you to be doing something constructive as opposed to fuming over how long the line is.)

Or imagine yourself in the aisle of a supermarket, finding the whatsit on your list at both waist level and just above your head. Take the latter. Take advantage of the opportunity to stretch the arm and the back. It was for this reason that I moved a can of coffee from a kitchen shelf that is an easy reach to the shelf above. Little things can mean a lot.

I have often been the object of strange glances on my walks through the streets of New York City because often when I come to a red light, if there's a corner building behind me, I take advantage of it: pushing against the wall, stretching the front of the thigh by pulling one leg up the back and then the other. (I'm always in running jogs.)

It isn't always a red light that prompts me to stop and stretch; sometimes it is the spot that calls, a spot where I feel that no one will observe me stretching. If someone happens upon me, surely I won't be recognized in my large dark glasses and wide-brimmed hat. So there I am in the swing of my stretching when time and again someone comes alongside me and says, "Hello, Miss Kitt!"—bringing us both to laughter. Caught in the act of stretching—there are worse things than that, yes? So why be shy about a chance to do your body a good turn?

There's housecleaning, too. I never thought that having housekeepers obligated me to do no housework. I have always done a fair amount when I could well afford to pay others to do it all (and having done domestic work as a teenager, I know how to clean a house).

I have yet to find an exercise greater than keeping a house. Washing dishes, cooking, making the bed, vacuuming, mopping, sweeping, dusting, moving furniture—every sort of movement is included in this job: lifting, pulling, pushing, bending, twisting, elevating, stretching. Your home can be a great gym. The mind gets its fair share, too: there's all sorts of figuring out that goes on when you clean a house.

Adventures and revitalizing challenges await you. Look for them in your everyday doings. I think you'll find no shortage of opportunities to stretch. I have found that the more I am interested in a healthy state, the more I want to stretch myself into doing things I do not feel like doing at a given moment. Sometimes, I do not feel like walking my dogs, for example. When I stretch myself and do it, I am always the better for having done so. There have been days when I have felt so out of sorts that I have heard myself saying, "I can't do the show tonight. I just don't have the energy." The moment I stretch myself to do it, the moment I walk into the room or out onto the stage—I am up, up, up. Pushing yourself to do when you do not feel like doing can give you the vigor to seek extraordinary ways to stretch yourself.

One of my greatest desires is to walk the Appalachian Trail, even now at my age. I want to see the beauty of the trail and challenge the body's ability—to see how well I have done in caring for it.

Brainstorm on prospects for mental and physical stretching that are in plain view or in easy access (and then follow up on the impulse).

1. _____

2. _____

3. _____

4. _____

5. _____

6. _____

7. _____

8. _____

9. _____

10. _____

THREE

Bend

With ease, bend over as far as you can to unhinge.

Savor the stretching of the back of your thighs.

Let your arms flow freely—be a rag doll—as you sway from side to side to loosen the hip area and to allow the mind to think of what the body is feeling: how the oxygen is flowing into different areas to burn fat, heal, and give life's fuel. Concentrate on the sections of yourself. Try to breathe life into every area. Think of self-healing, cleaning, strengthening, purifying. Take the oxygen into the brain area. Think. Concentrate. Repeat at least twice.

"Do you consider yourself a rigid person?"

"No," I replied. "I am very flexible—but only for my own needs, my own desires."

The interviewer seemed bewildered. My words gave me pause as well. Then I realized that I was not talking out of both sides of my mouth, for the idea of "my own needs, my own desires" is broad, encompassing much.

My overwhelming need and desire has been to survive, and this has required me to bend.

Imagine yourself at the edge of an ocean as a huge wave approaches. You have a choice: you can stand your ground or you can bend (duck or retreat to the beach). The question is, what is the greater need? To defy the wave or to survive it?

I certainly had to bend when a young man tried to force himself on me when I was a teenager. This was in central Harlem, in a house in which I had a room.

This fellow, whom I'd seen around the neighborhood, had gotten his foot in the door by telling me he had come to see another tenant (who wasn't in). Long story short: with no one else in the house, I was trapped. He warned me that there was no escape because his "boys" were outside on the stoop.

I was strong, but not strong enough to fight him and his "boys." Plus, he had a knife. So I bent.

I bent by stroking his ego, flattering him into believing that force was not necessary. I also convinced him that it would be better if we used some protection. When I told him I had something upstairs in the bathroom—which meant I had to go into the hallway of this rooming house—he let me go get it.

I walked up the stairs—quick, heavy steps. Then, as quiet as a mouse I tiptoed back down and eased out the front door. Casually, I walked through the knot of boys, and when I reached the corner, I ran like a bat out of hell.

Thank goodness I was nimble of mind and body. Thank goodness I thought to bend.

Frequently, bending to my own tide has meant following the call of conscience to be unyielding. Such was the case when I was performing at a swanky hotel in Swaziland in the 1970s.

By the time my engagement there was coming to an end, I had made friends with many of the maids who worked in the hotel, and they very much wanted to see my show.

"Surely, there's something we can do," I said to the maître d'.

"We'll see if we can find room for them," he said, "but we are completely sold out."

Since the maître d' said, "We'll see," I did not let the matter drop.

Daily, I followed up.

Daily, I was disappointed.

"Surely something can be done," I kept thinking.

Finally, softly, gently, and smiling, I said to the maître d', "Well, perhaps if there is no room for them, maybe there won't be room for me."

On the morning of my last show—

"Did you find places for the girls?"

Again—disappointment.

"Well, I guess there won't be a show tonight."

Would someone bend?

And there they were—ringside—as I walked out in dignity and pride with a smile on my face and in my heart and soul. The girls were glorious in their native costumes, hair done up in special-occasion designs, and bare feet.

Harry, my agent at the time, was a champ. Not only did he sit with them, but when he danced with them, others came over to make the same request. Tension was released. There was champagne all around and a good time was had by all who didn't let themselves get bent out of shape because things weren't as they were "supposed" to be.

On that fantastic night, all the "supposeds" were cast aside, as a consequence of bending. Had I bent and the maître d' not bent, it would not have gone well with my soul—and I would think not with his.

Similarly, it would not have been beneficial to me had I heeded the advice a doctor handed out when I was up in my forties and living in California.

"You are overdoing it. You are putting yourself in jeopardy." So said the good doctor when, during a checkup, I told him of the level of exercise I was accustomed to doing. It was a routine that included swimming, squash, stretching, and running five or so miles in the morning along the beach. Very often more.

"Don't you know that at your age you're not supposed to be doing things like that?"

It can be quite discombobulating when someone—especially an authority—tells you that you cannot do something that you are perfectly capable of doing and that you are doing perfectly well.

The good doctor's criticism of my workout was not only baffling, but also dispiriting. All of a sudden, *everything* started aching—but that didn't last long.

My instincts had served me well thus far. I saw no reason to dismiss them now. I decided that I was not going to let this physician put me in a box and label me too old for this and that. I went back to doing my thing, beach runs and all.

My lifelong commitment to exercise has necessitated some inflexibility. For instance, it is a rare day that I do not exercise in the morning, no matter where I am—at home, in a hotel, wherever, even if it's only stretching.

Rejuvenate! (It's Never Too Late)

I am firm about this morning ritual: from the long years of being in tune with my body, I know that my body and my mind will serve me best throughout the day if at the top of my day there is exercise of some sort.

Yes, we need to be relatively unyielding when it comes to the essentials: adequate rest, appropriate and properly executed exercise, eating habits that enhance the mind and the body (and let's not forget matters of conscience). As for the etcetera of our lives, we do well to do some bending so our minds and spirits do not become stiff and brittle by not allowing other thoughts to come in, by not having debates with those who do not agree with us. Aging becomes a real bore and a burden if we take the position that being set in our ways is a good thing, a badge of honor. (Age itself is a badge of honor to be respected, and its knowledge shared, used, respected.)

Habit, tradition—this can be good, but not just because of habit or tradition.

Why do some of us persist in wearing high-heeled shoes, especially those with pointed toes? Youth was once the reason. But now? Ought not bending to the need to not torture the feet take priority over bending to the desire to be fashionable? Is health not more important—no matter how young we are?

The "my way" approach to life and the stubborn adherence to traditions that have long since ceased to make sense—this, I think, can be unhealthy, impractical, and not logical. Intransigence on matters of no great consequence for no good reason reflects calcification and a spiritual-mental laziness.

Bending, on the other hand, can revitalize. Actually, sometimes we need to be flexible to find out where we really need to be rigid. If you keep yourself in a box, if you refuse to change some of your ways "just because," you may cease to learn and miss out on a lot—perhaps how to take care of yourself physically, how to stay mentally alert, a better way to enjoy *you*. My performances, for instance, are never the same. I bend to my feelings of the moment and to the feeling—what we call vibrations—from the audience.

A part of bending to my own tide involves yielding to my changing capabilities. When I was younger, I could run for miles along a California beach, and while living in a New York City high-rise, when returning to my apartment after a game of squash or tennis or a workout in Central Park or a gym, I would make a point of not taking the elevator up because taking the stairs up to the nineteenth floor would be a challenge and a workout: strengthening my thighs and lungs.

But we do change with time. While I am capable, in my seventies, of a level of calisthenics, yes, I have slowed down.

Too often, when we think about being "not as young as I used to be," we can end up depressed about what we cannot do to the point that we do *nothing*. Far better to have gratitude and a respectful attitude toward what we are capable of doing. This is bending to your own tide. This is being true and good to yourself, and it can bring you into a new appreciation of doing.

Take my dogs, Aba and Mutzi. I have come to appreciate them for more than the positive energy they emit. I am grateful for their needs—walking, feeding, grooming. Their needs give me the means to satisfy my need to keep mobile, to keep doing.

Something as mundane as opening a can of food for my dogs becomes an exercise. I make sure that I am standing correctly as I take the can opener to the can. I inhale deeply as I press the blade into the can. I exhale fully as I turn the knob.

Consider how an electric can opener would deprive me of the privilege of exercising! As long as I can use a manual can opener, I'm happy.

Dog-walking helps me keep fit, too. Aba and Mutzi are life-savers, particularly when I am not gung ho about going for a walk: their need motivates me when I do not feel like doing it. When I do, I definitely do my body a good turn. (It is so life-enhancing to have a little responsibility when you are in a position to be absolutely carefree. Retirees who take up a part-time job or engage in semiregular volunteer work understand well that a life of too much loose leisure and lounging deadens the mind and weakens the body.)

In yielding to the changes that come with age, I have become all the more adamant about seizing opportunities to attend to my body when all I have is my body to work with.

I am extracareful to not hunch over as I stir a pot and to not pitch forward as I walk up stairs. And there's the going up and down on my toes and pressing my buttocks together when I am standing in a line, at a red light, or at my kitchen sink. While I'm doing whatever, I am checking myself: "Is the stomach tight? Is the breathing correct?"

I see a spot on the kitchen floor or the loading of the dishwasher as an excellent opportunity to do a proper squat (back straight as I descend and rise, strengthening the thighs and not straining the back). In taxicabs, in an elevator, and in all sorts of places I'm so often doing some type of isometrics.

"Have you done this all your life? Every time I turn around you're exercising!"

That was George Wolfe in early 2000 during a rehearsal for *The Wild Party.* Darling, effervescent George wasn't yelling at me; he was merely registering his concern that I might not be giving full attention to his notes if I was stretching, bending, and doing the up-and-down on my toes while he talked.

To the contrary, I assured George. "My body has to be moving while my brain is analyzing what you say."

George came to understand that my bending to my own needs, my own desires, was of benefit to us both, and therefore to the show, a show that required me to do much bending.

First off, while I was playing one of the leads (Dolores), I was not the *main* character. Many performers who are accustomed to being number one seem to have trouble handling that kind of situation (or their managers do). But I have never measured success by where my name was on the marquee. To my mind, when I am doing my best, I am at number-oneness. So I was certainly not going to pass on a wonderfully challenging play such as *The Wild Party* merely because I wouldn't be the main character.

Fulfilling my desire to be a part of *The Wild Party* meant bending to a demanding rehearsal schedule. As is the case with doing any play, I also had to bend to what comes with the territory of working ensemble.

When I am doing my concerts, I have freedom when it comes to such matters as timing, which works off the spirit of the room at a particular moment. For instance, I may hold a note much longer than usual. Thankfully, my fabulous pianist and conductor, Darryl Waters, is up to bending with my flow (watching the back of my neck to see if I'm going to breathe, which tells him that I am about to go into the next phrase).

In contrast, when I am doing a play, I cannot do, to any extreme, as the spirit moves me. My timing must be in sync with what the director has laid out. I have to be considerate of the timing of the entire show, of my fellow actors, of the lighting cues: working with everyone else and not against them.

As I have ample opportunity to do my own thing in my

concerts, it is not a burden for me to do the bending required of a play (especially one with a sizable cast). In fact, it is a terrific challenge and exercise for me, since I've worked as a solo artist for most of my years in show business.

My work in *The Wild Party* involved bending with others in the show when we weren't before the audience. As the cast member with the most performance experience and the most years on earth, I naturally bent to youth as I fulfilled the role that I think elders are supposed to play: that of teacher and guide. I did this by just being me.

The bending that I was willing to do with regard to *The Wild Party* paid off handsomely in many ways, not the least of which was playing Dolores, the world-savvy but not world-weary elder in a group of show biz folks. Like me, Dolores has seen many a wild party in her day; yet, she has not frittered away her talents chasing the glitter life: she has not lost her way—and she has aged very well. She allowed herself to age naturally, letting nature take her course, without fear, just bending to her own tide and to the seasons of her life.

Make a list of things about which you know you have been needlessly inflexible.

1. _____

2. _____

3. _____

4. _____

5. _____

6. _____

7. _____

8. _____

9. _____

10. _____

FOUR

Rock-and-Roll

Lie on your back and hold your knees up loosely with your hands. Rock up and down—easily—holding your stomach tight. Rock about ten times, then pause and repeat, pause and repeat.

Next, stretch your body on the floor for as long as possible. Then, roll over and over.

I find that rocking-and-rolling is good for control and circulation.

"Go along to get along." Sometimes there is sense to that. Yet, those who adhere to this principle in excess can lose their way.

Get along? With whom? Will he or she (or they) enhance you in some way? Can you enhance them?

Get along? To where? When you have gone along, will you end up in a place you really want to be? And will you feel comfortable in that place?

Rebellion can be healthy, I have found. Rocking against what is an outrage to your being and rolling with your flow (or whatever you have to work with at a given moment) enables you to maintain your identity and individuality. It clarifies you and keeps you in touch with your essence. Rebellion is isometrics for the soul.

Some regard rebellion as the province of youth. I think otherwise. Actually, the older we get, the more we may need to rebel because with age comes greater temptation to complacency and contentment with the status quo.

I cannot say that I was "born to rebel," but I do know that all my life I have been prone to rebel, and what I have rebelled against can be summed up in one word: *stupidity.*

So, early on in my career, I said no to an agent who tried to talk me into passing myself off as Burmese or some other kind of "exotic"—something other than what I am: a woman of color out of the cotton fields of South Carolina.

But did my origins mean that I ought to limit myself to one style of music—or one style of anything?

"I'm going to make you the biggest blues singer in the world!" declared a record company executive.

I did not want to be a blues singer. Yes, I can sing the blues, but I did not want to be pigeonholed into one style of music because I did not grow up steeped in one style of music. (Besides, there were singers far better at the blues than I could ever be, I thought.)

I wanted to sing the songs I liked, which gave rise to a multicultural, international repertoire. How I delighted in the ability to communicate with different cultures, to bring a bit of songs American-style to people around the world, and to share with American audiences the sounds of other cultures. Being true to my delight meant that I rebelled against the notion that a woman of color had no business singing out of her culture.

"What's all this foreign-language stuff?" blurted out someone sitting right down front at Manhattan's La Vie En Rose. The bombshell hurt, but I was not about to let anyone kill my desire to be the artist I was intended to be. So I rolled on with "Uska Dara," which I had learned in Turkey, "C'est Si Bon," which I had learned in Paris, and other "foreign-language stuff." (*Stuff*—oh, how I dislike that word: so annoying, so vapid, so stupid, I think.)

I have rebelled against stupid isms offstage as well. Sometimes, it's been quite overt, as when I spent time on a beach in Capetown with an interracial group of children when apartheid was in full effect. And there was my journey from New York City to South Carolina to bury my aunt.

I had been away from America for some time and was not

in a race-terrorized state of mind. Accustomed as I was by then to first-class travel, I thought nothing of buying a first-class train ticket.

"You don't belong here," grunted the conductor when the train crossed the Mason-Dixon Line. "You have to move."

I didn't think anything of it, except that the law was stupid. So I stayed in the first-class car, pretending I did not understand a word he was saying. (When it comes to my rebellions against the stupidity of race and class prejudice, the half has not been told.)

On countless occasions I have rebelled against witless little rules that are not as damaging as the big isms, but are nevertheless irksome and inconvenient.

"I'm sorry, Miss Kitt, you can't come in because you're wearing pants," said the maître d' of a restaurant in Canada, where I was to lunch with a friend (the choice of restaurant, hers). I was not sporting dungarees or some other kind of casual pants. I was dressed respectably, looking quite glamorous, in fact, in my nice slacks, a silk blouse, and a three-quarter-length mink coat. Doesn't that sound like a sensible outfit for a Canadian winter day?

I did not think there would be any point in arguing with

the maître d'. Without a word, I about-faced, walked past the coat check and into the ladies' room, where I removed my pants. I then checked my slacks and proceeded to the dining room and was duly seated. The sight of me dining in a fur coat (legs crossed, of course) got far more notice than had I been dining in slacks.

I encountered similar nonsense when, during an engagement in the 1950s at the Plaza Hotel's Persian Room, my boyfriend and I dropped in at the bar in the Pierre Hotel diagonally across the street from the Plaza.

It was a gorgeous summer early evening, and I looked as if I had just stepped out of *Vogue*—black silk cocktail dress, with matching bag and sandals, hair exquisitely coiffed.

"I'm sorry, Miss Kitt, but you can't come in because you don't have stockings on," said the maître d'.

I looked down at my clean and pedicured feet in those gorgeous sandals, and I thought, "How stupid!"

"How do you know that I do not have any stockings on?"

"I can tell by your toes."

"What kind of law is that?"

"That's the law."

"What a stupid law!"

The maître d' shrugged. "All I know is, you can't come in."

So I went to the hotel's shop and bought a pair of stockings (they were singles at the time), which I put on but did not roll up.

When I returned to the dining room, the maître d' just looked at me and shrugged his shoulders.

"Well," I remarked, "you said I had to wear stockings, but you did not tell me how I should wear them."

As the waiter led my boyfriend and me to a table, people were thinking I don't know what at the sight of my stockings flapping around my ankles.

Such small acts of rebellion set some minds to thinking me a little troublemaker or a little nuts. But I have never rebelled because I wanted to be evil, never rocked the boat simply to make waves. Rebellion for the hell of it is just another kind of stupidity (unless, perhaps, you're a kid in the grip of growing pains). When I have defied a rule, I have done so to shed light on the nonsensical. Doing so has meant not concerning myself with what the ubiquitous "they" might say, but with making them, perhaps, think.

I had plenty of experience with that when it came to affairs of the heart. Love knows nothing about color. So I had to let a lot of stupidity roll off my back when I dated John Barry Ryan III, Arthur Loew Jr., Charlie Revson, and other white men—and when I married a white man, didn't that give a lot of people conniptions. (And when my marriage to Bill McDonald ended, I rebelled against the notion that I should remarry simply to "save" myself from the stigma of *divorcée*.)

My most everyday (and everlasting) act of rebellion is against being a slave to the marketplace. When Eartha was the only person I had to take care of, I resisted being a silly consumer for the sake of my finances and for conscience' sake. When I became a mother, I had another reason: to teach my daughter that things do not bring lasting happiness.

It is difficult not to spoil your children. At times I was not successful in rebelling against that impulse all parents occasionally have to buy their children's affections.

I went through the Barbie doll syndrome, until one day I realized that I was being manipulated by the marketplace through my child. I became ashamed that I had allowed this to happen. (And who knows what happened to that Barbie doll that Kitt just *had* to have, and to Barbie's wardrobe—she was often dressed better than I.)

There was a time when I was not in such great shape financially. Compared with millions of people, Kitt and I were living well, but I needed to step back from the standard to which we were accustomed. Though I never bothered Kitt with my financial woes, I knew she knew that something was off the beat of our lives. Yet, when she told me she wanted her bedroom redone—with a chart of all the new things she wanted me to buy—I relented. I managed to get up the money to abide by her wishes, trying (stupidly) to show her that all was well.

I did not like the room when it was finished. Even now I have a suspicion that she did not like the room either. So what did I achieve? I should have sat my daughter down and said, "We have to do with what I can afford right now. So let's do your room up with what we have. Let's challenge ourselves." Kitt was fifteen. She was perfectly capable of understanding an explained problem.

What has this to do with your well-being? Spoil a child today and tomorrow you may have headaches and heartaches galore. When we rebel against Madison Avenue, we spare ourselves a lot of stress in terms of our finances and the character of our children (and grandchildren).

* * *

When you rebel, sometimes there is a price to pay; but I believe that the price we pay for being true to ourselves is worth it: worth the slander, the ostracism, the tsk-tsks we may endure for a time when we refuse to go along to get along. For if we endure, we are stronger. Of that, I am a witness.

As you may have guessed, I am thinking here of my most "famous" act of rebellion: my speaking truth to power in 1968 at a White House luncheon hosted by Lady Bird Johnson. Ironically, I was not thinking myself rebellious at all. In fact, I thought I was going along with the program: an inquiry into teenage delinquency in America.

Because of my work with children in Watts and elsewhere in America and the world, the thinking was that I would be an asset to the discussion of teenage delinquency in America. And my thinking was that they wanted my honest opinion when it came to the question "Why is there so much delinquency in the streets of America?"

I said what I felt to be true: that the war in Vietnam had a lot to do with it. I recounted conversations in dressing rooms in different parts of the world with bright, beautiful young men. They were young men fleeing the draft who sincerely believed, as did I, that the war was unfair, nonsensical, unwinnable, with horrendous slaughter of the innocents on both sides. I also said that I knew of good boys who did bad things that would get them a little jail time (such as smoking pot) in order not to get sent to Vietnam. "You send the best of this country off to be shot and maimed. No wonder the kids rebel and take pot." Could we really blame young people for wanting to go to sleep until the war ended?

When I sat down, a woman remarked, "Miss Kitt, I'll have you know that I have eight sons and I'd be glad to donate each one of them to Vietnam."

"Then how can I talk to you?" was my response.

In sweet contrast, a woman seated next to me bowed her head, put her hand on my knee, and said, "Thank you for saying what you did. We all feel the same way, but seventy-five percent of the women at this luncheon are wives of men who work for President Johnson."

I don't think anyone said anything to me after that. It was as if the room had taken a breath and forgotten to exhale.

Strange things began to happen and to not happen. First off, whereas the White House had arranged for a car to bring me to the luncheon, there was no car for me when the luncheon was over.

By the time I got back to my hotel (by cab), the incident had hit the press.

"Don't say anything to anybody, just get on a plane and come home as soon as possible!" urged my secretary in Beverly Hills. Hers was the first call I got.

There were more calls and more calls, and I was thrown on television, up against the wall to explain myself and to apologize for having made the first lady cry. (I hadn't seen her cry.)

When I returned to Los Angeles—big press conference, and more pressure to apologize to Lady Bird Johnson.

"I don't see any reason why I should apologize to her; she should be apologizing to the young boys of this country who are being sent off to a war they don't want to be involved in."

The drama went on for another few weeks. Some of it, I must say, was quite touching: for instance, the teenagers who went through the streets shouting, "Eartha Kitt for president! Eartha Kitt for president!" (The Sunday after the luncheon, one group took the chant down the aisles of the church where the Johnsons worshiped.)

I was like a prisoner in my own house for a time. When it was "safe" to go outside, things got quite odd.

Rejuvenate! (It's Never Too Late)

All across the country, engagements—at hotels, in clubs, and on television shows—canceled! (I will never forget the goodness and courage of Paul Sonnebend of the Plaza Hotel: he continued to hire me when I was persona non grata.)

At the time, I was not aware of the depth of the government's wrath. I chalked the cancellations and the no-calls up to a waning in my popularity, and I rolled with it. Abroad, people wanted me, so I went where the work was, surviving for myself and my daughter.

Not until January 1974 did I discover that I had been the target of government persecution. The messenger was Seymour Hirsch, who called to ask permission to print, in a *New York Times* article, the dossier the CIA had compiled on me. Nymphomania was in this catalog of "information"—all of it untruths born of backyard gossip.

I was between laughter and tears as I listened to Seymour. I could not believe that my government would seek to ruin me. All the time that I worked abroad, America remained "home." After I found out about the government's efforts to destroy me, I never stopped loving my country, and to this day I do not regret having said what I said at that White House luncheon. The truth shall set you free (and I still have hopes for America).

When America opened her arms to me again—Jimmy Carter's invitation to the White House in 1978 to *Timbuktu!* and beyond—I rolled with it all, too grateful to be bitter.

I have kept rocking, too. For one, I rock against the notion that age is a disease, a pity, something to fight mightily, even to the point of extreme measures to "recapture youth." I am so grateful to have seen fifty, sixty, seventy—and to be in relatively good health at that! Why would I want to deny my age or try to hide it? If the gods let me see eighty, ninety, one hundred—I will shout my age from the rooftops while doing my belly dance.

Taking care of myself, through proper diet and ongoing exercise of my mind and body—this is my focus, not trying to fool myself or anybody else that I am any younger than I am. What would be the point? That kind of thinking makes you vulnerable to being conned into believing that such-and-such pot of cream will make you look twenty years younger. (That may be so, but you won't be twenty years younger.) It amazes me that some people spend more time and energy on fountainof-youth products and procedures for the surface self than they do on healthy eating and right exercise for the inner self.

My respect for aging, my embrace of it as a natural process, made me rock against the rocking chair. Sixty . . . sixty-five . . . seventy—retirement? *Monotonous!* As long as the public wants me and as long as I am capable of doing what I do, why not?

I think that not until the age of sixty (or thereabouts) do we fully realize our value—and we want to share it (or at least I think one ought to). For some, this epiphany may come in their forties or fifties. All I know is that it wasn't until I was in my sixties that I came into a fierce appreciation of myself— particularly as a person who had succeeded against the odds, who had not given up. This new appreciation and celebration of myself spurs me to keep doing the thing I so love to do, and to teach and to share in various ways, such as through this book.

How can you pass on the wisdom that has come with the years if you devote great quantities of days to fishing or creak-ing in a rocking chair with a scrapbook on your lap?

By the way, I do have a rocking chair. I find it stress-relieving to sit in this chair and rock . . . rock . . . rock, thinking to the rhythm I create, thinking about the rocking-and-rolling I have done over the years and recollecting how this "exercise" has kept me in touch with who I am, alive to myself and thus alive to life. This makes me feel so glad that I have never looked outside myself for my mental health.

Surrender to a shrink—that's another thing I rocked against when my mind and soul were troubled. To talk to a therapist once in a while can be helpful (and I've done that), but a lifetime of sessions would have left me insane, I think. It would not have been healthy for me in the long run to pay someone one or two times a week to tell me what I already know or to convince me that I am not honest enough with myself. When we find ourselves in a quandary or in a pit, isn't that what friends are for? If you do not have friends to whom you can talk out your problems at times, then you do not have friends, in which case you might want to make some.

And what if I am a little crazy? There's no one who can show Eartha how to make creative, constructive use of it better than Eartha. Anyway, I happen to think a little insanity is a good thing. Aren't we all a bit "off" because we are all different, fabulously unique? Yet, oftentimes, we skip our natural beat for the sake of being accepted. It is really the ubiquitous "they" who make you feel that you are crazy, wrong, don't belong. We can become unhealthy and perhaps even harmful to ourselves and others when we go along to get along for no good reason, when we do not rebel at least once in a while.

Are there areas in your life where you know in your soul that you are long overdue for a little rock-and-roll?

1. _____

2. _____

3. _____

4. _____

5. _____

6. _____

7. _____

8. _____

9. _____

10. _____

FIVE

Release

Get down on your hands and knees in a catlike position. Contract and release the center of your body.

Do this for as long as you can at one time (try ten times, with two repeats). As you do the exercise, breathe with the stomach acting as a balloon: breathe in as the body pulls up, breathe out as you release—stomach tight!

If you do this exercise your back and stomach muscles will thank you.

We all know how vital it is for the body to eliminate, to release what it does not need. The prudent, therefore, take care of the colon through proper diet and, if necessary, through extraordinary means such as the colonic.

The cleaner the colon, the better the body.

The cleaner we keep the noncorporeal self, the better our lives (the body included, for a clogged, cluttered, and unclean mind-spirit-soul can wreak havoc on the body). And how do we keep our essential selves clean? For starters, by releasing the desire for things that we do not need.

Having begun life in poverty, and having been the starving artist for a time, I was a prime candidate for becoming madly materialistic when my income began to exceed my dreams.

Nudging me on to unbridled acquisition were associates and "friends."

I did my share of spending on nonessentials. I was no stranger to extravagances, to the splurge. I always, however, saw a home, an automobile, and warm clothing as *needs.* I never allowed nonessential possessions to possess me.

Observation kept me in check. Among the superwealthy people I came to know and spend time with, some were not corrupted by their possessions. Others were.

The possession-obsessed people did not have a peace about what they had: they worried about *keeping* what they had accumulated; they worried about accumulating more and more and more. It was misery-making.

Along with real-life examples of materialism, I had as a teacher the many folktales, sacred texts, and other writings that speak to the problems that come of confusing need with greed.

Keeping me clean of greed, too, is my lifelong fascination with animals. I have learned so much from them: the farm animals I tended as a child; the wild animals I watched in my place of solace, the woods; the familiar and exotic creatures I encountered in distant lands.

The animal who kills for any reason other than sustenance or in defense of self and family is an aberration. The normal carnivore will walk away from the "table" when sated, even though a great amount of meat remains on the carcass. Birds gather only the amount of straw and twig needed to build the nest. When we find hoarding in the animal world, it is when the creatures—bears, bees, birds, squirrels—are readying themselves for winter.

With the years, I have acquired less and less. Rarely do I buy something that I do not need. (When I do buy something, often the purchase is not really for me but rather is something that I believe my daughter or my grandchildren will later on enjoy and cherish.) Nor do I care to receive things that I do not need. Take jewelry. Other than for publicity purposes, I do not wear jewelry. There was a time when I had many exquisite pieces—all gifts from friends and lovers. I loved having the jewelry, loved wearing it, too. Almost all of it ended up out of my hands, however: stolen by strangers, and a few pieces by friends. It turned out to be quite a relief. For when it was gone, I realized that I did not need the jewelry: keeping it insured and doing all the safekeeping (which turned out to be in vain anyway) was really a burden. And I would always have the memory of the people who had given the gems and precious metals. So a diamond is not this girl's best friend. If today someone were to give me a million-dollar diamond, oh, yes, I would be most appreciative, but if truth be told, I'd probably hock it and with the money buy real estate. I understand the dirt and can create good things with land, whereas all I can do with a diamond is wear it—stressed constantly that someone will rob me of it, and stressed that the insurance is costly.

I have pretty much the same outlook on clothing as I do on jewelry. I do not need a closetful of clothes. In my everyday doings, I am content to wear practically the same few items all the time. I am concerned about comfort, not about being fashionable. Being content with a simple wardrobe greatly frees me up: the more clothes one has, the more there is to take care of, to keep track of, and to accessorize. Too much choice can be stressful. What's more, an abundance of things costs money, and I think there are more worthwhile ways to spend money.

And why not perform in the same dress again and again? At my concerts my focus is to perform to the best of my abilities, not to give a fashion show. Several changes of clothing during a show would hardly improve my talents. What matters to me is how a dress supports an act: that it allows me to move my legs and the rest of my body as I want. So I only need to purchase one or two new dresses a year for my work, thereby releasing the stress of whether the audience came to see me or my gowns.

What I care to hold on to are those things that have lasting value: those things that carry with them invigorating memories. At a glance, my mind can exercise—recollecting the who, what, when, where, and why of the object as it carries the spirit of happiness.

I have an Egyptianesque vase with a serpent winding round. This was a gift from the artist who created it, Sara, the aunt of Jessica Grové, a castmate in *The Wizard of Oz*. When I look at this vase, I remember my visit to the artist's home. I remember that she did not try to sell me any of her wares. She noticed my admiration of one item in particular, and she followed her impulse to give. When I look at this vase, I can feel its value: the artist's spirit is in it, her soul, her love of her art. There is value, too, in the memory of the good feeling in her surroundings and in her. Her spirit caressed her abode and welcomed those who entered.

It was the same with the Chinese gentleman in Burma, Mr. Kwong, who gave me a painting of a Burmese dancer when I dined with him and his family. It was the same with the Scotsman who gave me a Scottish love letter: a piece of wood, about a hand wide and a foot long, with hearts and leaves carved into it. Once upon a time, a suitor would leave such a love letter at the door of the pursued; if she accepted it, she was saying yes to his desire to court her. Then, too, there's the painting given to me by a Karachi miniaturist (the last of his kind). This piece hangs at the entrance of my bedroom. When I see it as I enter my room to sleep, I remember Karachi and Bazard and his beloved, and I sleep with love in my soul. Thusly, I wake up with less stress.

Possessions such as the vase, the dancer painting, the Scottish love letter, and the Karachi miniature are true to the meaning of *souvenir.* They really do "call to mind." As does the skull of July, the Saint Bernard I had many years ago.

Some might find the sight of July's skull unnerving, because skulls bring to mind death. Yet, when I look at July's skull, I do not think only of his passing; I think also of his life, and the delight he brought to my life: the moments we shared walking in the woods and along the roadways. July disappeared one day, and I found his skull where we used to sit to rest and to think. And now July's skull rests on a shelf in my home.

Much good can come of holding on to things that hold memories of special people, places, and experiences. This is why, though I greatly appreciate the gift of cut flowers, I often think, "Oh, would that it were a plant!" Cut flowers die and must be discarded. Although I do not let the decayed flowers go to waste (they become compost), they are gone from view and therefore cannot "call to mind." With a plant, when I water it or pass it by, my mind gets yet another chance to work, to remember. The occasion. The giver. How tall was it when it arrived? And there's the caring for the plant, giving me another occasion to exercise my mind and my body.

A great deal of accumulating is often motivated by the desire to impress and to be envied, both of which I regard as a poor use of time and energy. For some, release from reckless, fruitless acquisition and clinging to things can only come when they release the need to impress or to one-up.

Once you release these yearnings, you make yourself available to constructive things. It might be that your finances improve, and with that, your mood. (There's nothing like reducing debt to release some stress.)

I have also found that being unconcerned with status symbols and with impressing others—I can do that onstage—has brought me opportunities to utilize my mind and imagination, to be creative.

Around my kitchen table are five chairs that I found in a junk shop in New Milford, Connecticut. Seventy-five dollars for the lot of them. I spent $100 to have them stripped and painted a soft green that I adore. My needlepoint covers the seats.

Seeing through the junked state of the chairs was a workout for my mind. Creating the needlepoint for the seats was a workout for my mind and my hands. (And I had a glass breakfast table made so my artwork could be seen.)

I could have purchased a table and chairs from a ritzy, name-droppable shop. I could have spent thousands of dollars were I concerned with status, if I measured my worth by the cost of my possessions. But I'm not and I don't, and so I had a fantastic time rejuvenating the old—in more ways than one the body and mind working together.

People hold on to an abundance of purposeless things because they never want to let go. Perhaps there's some fear of future want. "Never know when I might need that," the thinking goes.

Release. Release what no longer serves a purpose in your life. Release what you do not need. Release and feel the renewal that comes when you recycle: when you give your extra to someone who can make use of it or to an organization that serves the needy. Consider, too, giving something you cherish to someone sure to cherish the item as much as, or perhaps more than, you do. I think of the pillows I made for my accountant and his assistant and the prayer rug I made for a friend. Sacrificial giving strengthens you. It releases you from fear of lack; so actually, it is really not a sacrifice at all.

When I was starting out in show business, there were days when the singers, actors, dancers, and other artists with whom I worked and palled around had little. Instead of keeping our little to ourselves, we shared: food, clothing, money. I feel that the good we do always returns: sometimes from a friend, sometimes from a stranger. We really do reap what we sow.

There is a harvest whether we share with a friend or a stranger. This brings to mind Marketplace Man, whom I met in Berlin. Actually, I never really "met" him: I never knew his name, never learned his story; no words ever passed between us. The point where we connected was a small garden square. I was living in an apartment on the square, while doing *Follies* at the Des Weston Theatre.

On Wednesdays and Saturdays the street became a marketplace, crowded with kiosks overflowing with produce, cooked food, handcrafted things, honey from the farms—the works.

What a delight it was to mill about, chatting with people I did not know, having a little taste of this and a bit of that— having an authentic cultural exchange. And one day I saw Marketplace Man.

He was not there to mill about and mingle, but to scavenge in the wastebaskets that hung from the lampposts.

I watched people watch him in his tattered soldier's garb. I watched people ignore him. Not even a piece of bread was offered.

On subsequent trips to the market I came with Marketplace Man in mind. I brought some food: some portion of what I had had in a restaurant or from the house of a cast member. I wrapped it up and even dressed it with a bit of ribbon. Then, I walked up ahead of him and placed the package of food in the basket he was sure to stop at next. "This is for you," read the note in German attached to the package.

One night, while walking about the square, about a half block from my rooms, I came upon Marketplace Man on a bench. He was covered up, asleep.

I got into the habit of bringing him food at night: something I had cooked, or something from a friend's kitchen or from the restaurant at which I had eaten. For nights, I stopped by Marketplace Man's "rooms" and left a package of food by his side or on top of his stomach. This lasted for three months, until *Follies* closed.

Taking on this responsibility of sharing with a stranger in need massaged my soul and made my spirit fly. I was happy with myself and enjoyed the memory of teenaged Eartha Mae (having run away from her aunt) picking through the garbage cans of New York City and swiping people's leavings from the Horn and Hardart. (I greatly miss the Horn and Hardarts.)

* * *

We revitalize not only when we give of ourselves to people, but also when we give of ourselves to the rest of Creation. I encourage everyone (especially those who live alone) to have a pet—a dog, a cat, parakeets, a little turtle, some fish. If an animal is not feasible, consider plants. (The Pet Rock was not as silly as some thought. It served to make you wonder how such a stupid idea could become such a need for people to buy and be responsible for. It also made you think, "How can I get a stupid idea like that and get rich?")

Having a pet not only gives you cause to exercise your mind and body, it also can cause you to exercise your spirit. You are being kind, tender, thoughtful, loving. When we release such energies, we renew ourselves.

The birds who live near me know that they can always get a bite to eat at my house, from the bird feeder I mainly stock with sunflower seeds, along with suet in the winter. When preparing to go out of town, uppermost in my mind is arranging for my daughter or a neighbor to tend to the bird feeder (and water the plants).

From the energy I expend for the benefit of the birds, I get the benefit of beholding their marvelous colors and movements all the closer; and their song comes all the nearer to my ears. Watching them, inevitably, gets me pondering, thinking—working the mind. Where do they sleep? How do they keep warm when it's cold?

Mr. Cardinal . . . see how he sits on the branch for a while before he darts to the feeder? He is checking out the scene, I deduce. He is making sure that no enemies lurk. Yes, I think, how very important it is that we look before we leap. I think of the mishaps and misfortunes that can come of haste.

People often make fun of or label "crazy" elderly people who sit on park benches and feed the birds: thinking, passing time in their memories, wondering who's going to take care of *them* when the need arrives. These bird feeders are not so crazy and hardly ridiculous. They are sharing, giving, keeping themselves connected.

In the pond out behind my house, I have three electrical irrigation systems circulating the water, keeping it oxygenated and clear of contamination. My care for the pond makes it attractive to all sorts of birds. It is amazing how many different families come yearly once the word gets around.

Sometimes I take my breakfast and sit by the pond watching the school of fish that I cannot eat (everything becomes a pet). When the flocks of birds come to share the pond, I analyze how the breeds section themselves off.

Oh, look, is that a crane?

When it's freezing cold, because my pond is not frozen—oh, how the wild birds come! Sometimes in the middle of winter, perhaps on their way South or on the return, they have come in droves some days. One day there were twenty, thirty, fifty mallards.

The ducks, the geese, that solitary crane—the sight of them invigorates me. As with Mr. Cardinal, watching the wildfowl gives me food for thought about the living of my life, as does the sight of the mourning doves keeping the peace, often mingling with the squirrels who feed on the throw-off from the bird feeder.

The more I watch the animals take care of themselves, the more I want to help them out, and to pass the mission along. That is why during one spring, for a while no one came in and out my front door. In this DO NOT DISTURB situation, some birds had made a duplex apartment in the wreath on the wall by the front door: one nest on the top of the wreath, another on the lower rim. They laid eggs that hatched. It was a great experience for my grandchildren, especially five-year-old Rachel, who loved to be lifted up to see the progress from eggs to chicks (and to see the mother caring for her babies). We missed the winged family after they left, at the same time that we were happy to see them go on with their lives.

Stress. This is something we absolutely need to release for the sake of our well-being. There is a saying I heard somewhere: "I'm too blessed to be stressed." I think of this saying often and count my blessings, and doing so greatly relieves me of the stress that might be creeping up on me.

Exercise is, of course, a major stress-reducer, safer and more effective than any pill or potion. (But if you're exercising out of sheer vanity, with the spirit of competition with others, exercise can become stressful as well.)

We also release stress when we let go of anger, hurts, and other unhealthy emotions. Remember chapter one: Inhale. Exhale. *Breathe!* Strongly, as though the oxygen from this breathing exercise can wash away the hurt, the anger, and any other unnecessary feelings. When you have been hurt by someone, don't fall into the trap of revenge. Karma will take care of that. Remember: what goes around . . . And the more you learn to release the negative, the more you will be able to use stress constructively. (Just before I go onstage, I am a nervous wreck; but I use it to fuel me into performing.)

In my pursuit of less stress, I have also found it helpful not to expect too much out of life. I hold to this even as I hold to the belief that something wonderful will happen. There's no contradiction here. Not expecting too much means that I do not pester the gods with a list, all the while that I stay ready to see and feel what is wonderful in what happens and in what does not happen. Great expectations can lead to great wanting, which can lure you into Faustian bargains. And make no mistake, the devil always gets his due—and if you try to shortchange him, he might take it all.

Begin a list of things you would like to release.

1. _____

2. _____

3. _____

4. _____

5. _____

6. _____

7. _____

8. _____

9. _____

10. _____

Six

Walk

Walking is the simplest thing in the world to do—and the best and cheapest form of aerobics (no fees, no equipment). But you must do it correctly. Inhale on one step and exhale on the other (or on every other step depending on your pace and rhythm). As you walk, keep your back straight and your shoulders over your hips, neither rearing back nor pitching forward. Constantly be aware of your breathing (stomach ballooning on the inhale, stomach going flat on the exhale).

There is a horror in unnecessary rushing: time flies and you're not having all that much fun. Are we hurrying to the coffin? Into more stress?

The speed with which some live their lives only strains and drains the body and the brain, leaving one frayed, jagged, fatigued, bewildered—what? It's Christmas again? Another birthday so soon? Where, oh, where did the summer go?

My advice? Don't speed when there's no need.

The quality of life is not to be found in how much we pack into every hour, every minute, but in how wisely we use the time we have. Often we make the best use of time when we walk through our tasks and experiences: at times briskly, at times at a stroll, but always with thought, purpose, and control. (Don't take the word *walk* to mean "lazily.")

Does technology play a part in this increasing need for speed? Rather, it's our abuse of technology, don't you think? Some of us have it all: the phone with call waiting and call forwarding, the fax, the cell phone, the car phone, the E-mail address at home and the E-mail address at work, the beeper, the PDA, et cetera, et cetera—and let us not forget the microwave that quickens the meals but shortens the life span with family or friends, perhaps. (Are we sure it does no harm?)

As we take on more gizmos and services (and more bills), we give scant thought to the toll these time-savers and expediters might take on our mental and emotional health. And a distressed mind and spirit debilitate the body.

Our era's needless speed and phantom urgency has had impact on so many aspects of our lives. There is the decline in the quality of conversation, for one. The art of listening seems to be going the way of the dinosaur. We are so in a hurry to respond that often we do not listen to the point raised or the question asked. As a consequence of our not listening, not thinking, not *walking* through an exchange, we often end up in conversations that might be ridiculous, and can sometimes be regrettable. What is so wrong with saying "I don't know" or "I'll have to think about that one" or "What do you mean? I don't understand"? A pause to listen is much better than babbling: it enables you to listen to the other person's words, body language, and silence (there's a lot to analyze in silence).

I resist high-speed conversations, unless there is some urgent need for them (like getting as much in as possible before the commercials when being interviewed on television). I prefer to make sense when I speak, and often that requires a little thought, which requires a little time, a pause.

It is not only our face-to-face conversations that get rushed. Our telephone conversations suffer as well (perhaps more so). Often, when I am on the phone with someone who is speeding (and repeating himself or herself), for the sake of my sanity I must simply pull back.

"Are you there?" asks the other party.

"Yes, I'm here." Again, I pause.

"Well?"

"I am thinking about what you said."

The other party's impatience is palpable, and I cannot help but infer that she does not really want to know what I think, does not really want to engage in a conversation. Or perhaps she is not interested in listening: she has talked on top of what was said and therefore did not hear what I said.

Maybe we take our cues from the fast talk on television. Perhaps most harmful of all to the health of private and public discourse are some of those "serious" gatherings of pundits and experts that purport to help viewers gain insight into the major issues and world events. Yet, hosts and guests often do not listen to one another. They interrupt each other shamelessly and appear more keen on getting in a zinger than making sense. What can careless viewers learn from that other than how to converse badly? I watch certain Sunday-morning news shows, but they agitate me so. Why do I watch them? Because you can learn a lot by analyzing what you do not like.

Another thing that I find disturbing is the sight of someone racing through a meal. We ought to walk—not run!—through our meals. Only if we take our time in eating will we chew properly (all the better for the digestion). Those counting the calories ought to remember, too, that the more *s-l-o-w-l-y* one eats, the *less* one eats.

I walk through meals for health, and for joy as well. I want to savor the flavors; I want to take in the way the food is plated and the way the different foods complement each other in color, texture, and taste. (I have long known that the more colorful the plate, the more vitamins I'm apt to obtain.) I also want to give myself time to consider the good that the food will do for my mind and my body. So I'm analyzing at every bite: How am I digesting this? Is this soothing to my taste buds? Is that contributing to my desire to be healthy? If eating means racing through a meal, unless I am desperate with hunger, I would rather not eat. Instead, I will, if possible, nibble on something, such as a piece of fruit or nuts.

Also among my druthers—"Sleep on it."

At times I have rushed into or out of a business matter because I succumbed to the pressure of an agent, manager, or friend, only to realize after I had slept on the matter that the yes or no to such and such a job, for example, was wrong for me. Although I have not had a perfect score when it comes to sleeping on a matter, over the years my average has improved and, as a consequence, the regrets are fewer.

A snap decision is not always a sign of a sharp mind or the ability to think on one's feet, as some would have us believe. Snap decisions are often a sign of a muddled state of mind. Decisiveness in and of itself is nothing to be praised, especially if it leads to woe later on down the road. Yet, at times a snap decision is right: when your mind is clear and you are in tune with your instincts.

The value I place on walking through meals, conversations, and other facets of living arises, in part, from lessons learned from actual walking, which is my number one exercise.

I have been a walker all of my life. When I was a child in the South, my feet were the only form of transportation I knew. When I was sent up North, I continued to walk a lot, even though New York City had a great public transportation system. Buses and subways cost money: with the ten cents I did not spend on downtown-uptown or crosstown round-trips, I could buy a hamburger or some kind of nourishment.

When money was not an issue, I continued to walk New York, knowing that I could frequently get from one place to another more quickly and with less stress than if I took the subway, the bus, or a taxi.

I have always been rather zealous about seizing opportunities to walk, often stretching myself and finding that the more I walked the more I could walk and the more I wanted to walk. For instance, when I was living on Eighty-seventh

Street in Manhattan, at one point I was teaching a dance class all the way down on Fourteenth Street. I stretched myself into walking the distance both ways. When I returned home, I walked up the nineteen flights of stairs to my apartment. My calves, thighs, and lungs benefited greatly. This walking was good for all of me, really, because walking also gives the mind and emotions a workout—if you walk in a state of curiosity, that is. Wherever I'm walking, I do so in anticipation of discovery, and I have rarely, if ever, been disappointed.

New York City is such a wonderful place for walks—so much to see. For me, one of the wonders is the architecture: so many styles, from Gothic to modern and beyond. I especially love the Old World buildings: monuments to fantastic design and craft, erected at a time when we did not have the kind of machinery that we now have with which to throw things up. Riding by in a bus or a taxi, I would not be able to behold grand creations such as the Plaza Hotel, Grand Central Station, the Empire State Building, the Dakota, or the Carlyle Hotel.

I have never been able to walk by Broadway and Thirty-ninth Street and not think of the original Metropolitan Opera House, and how few of us there are who remember that exquisite building. I think, too, how progress can bury memory. All the more reason for me to keep walking, letting the sights hone the thinking and tone the memory.

In Central Park, I once happened upon a tiny graveyard near the band shell. During other walks I have taken note of the number of cherry trees or birch trees I came across and wondered what is really planted in Strawberry Fields. Many a Sunday, while walking around a small pond, I have delighted in watching the byplay between fathers and young sons testing their little motorboats. When my dogs were along, as they got acquainted with the city dogs, I got acquainted with the city folks.

Walking by Belvedere Castle in Central Park calls to mind Errol Flynn's movies, which bring to mind the Garden of Allah Hotel, where I lived in the fall of 1953 while in Los Angeles doing *New Faces* at the Biltmore Theatre and headlining at the Mocombo in Beverly Hills. The hotel was where Errol Flynn had had many of his affairs and where I had many a chuckle over someone's recollection of Flynn's antics.

Thinking about that hotel prompts the memory of wonderful Charlie Morrison, the owner of the Mocombo. He had flown to Chicago when *New Faces* was there to ask me to quit the show for work at the Mocombo. "I need you, I need you," he pleaded, because, he said, he knew that if my name was on a contract to perform at his club, he would be able to get credit again with the liquor vendors (and thereby do more business and thereby get out of debt).

I wouldn't quit *New Faces,* but I promised Mr. Morrison that when the show got to Los Angeles, I would work at his club.

What a hectic month or two that was. On top of the Mocombo and *New Faces* (the show and the making of the film), I was also making records for RCA. My schedule was so tight that I hardly had time to breathe. As time was so of the essence, arrangements were made for the police to pick me up every night at the Biltmore. As soon as I came off the stage, a blanket was thrown around me and I was tossed into a patrol car that sped me up to the Mocombo, where I wasn't through until about three o'clock in the morning.

I ended up coming down with something (pneumonia or one of its relatives). But I had no regrets, other than the nasty comments Leonard Sillman made to the press that resulted in the newspaper headline "Eartha Kitt's Walkout on *New Faces* Gained Her No Friends." This and the illness were soothed by

Charlie Morrison's great kindness, such as on the day, while heeding the doctor's prescription of bed rest, I looked out my bungalow window and saw him and a handful of waiters coming my way with a bounty.

It was Thanksgiving Day—turkey and the works! Along with Dom Pérignon champagne, beluga caviar, perfume, a cashmere sweater or two, and a gold pounded cigarette case engraved with my name (a diamond dotting the *i*).

"We came to be sure that you ate today," said Charlie Morrison. "Without you we wouldn't have a business."

All that from a walk by Belvedere Castle in Central Park.

In Central Park, I have noticed paths that were not there when I was a kid. When I have walked north through the park, I have come to Harlem, where I have walked some more, remembering the places where I once lived, especially the second-floor apartment at 126 West 143rd Street, in which I lived with the Wayde family; remembering the shop long gone where Mrs. Wayde sent me to buy her silk stockings; remembering my walks to and from P.S. 119 and P.S. 136; remembering the country kid adjusting to city ways, which I don't think I ever did.

Given all the history and memories that a walk summons

up, we—parents, grandparents, aunts, uncles—do well to walk not only ourselves, but also the children in our lives, even if only to walk them around the block. (If you have no children in your life, perhaps there are friends who trust you with theirs.)

With two (or more) generations out for a walk the adults get good exercise as they share with the young memories of a place, as they cultivate within the young the value of walking and talking and being curious. From the children's questions and discoveries, the adults learn. Seeing things through a child's eyes can be invigorating, as my mother-in-law marveled one day when we were in Hong Kong. She was telling me the story behind the present of a stone that my daughter had just given me.

Gramma McDonald and three-year-old Kitt were out for a walk around the Mandarin Hotel block when Kitt came upon this heart-shaped stone on the sidewalk where some excavation was going on. Kitt and I were always playing in the dirt and forever picking things up and engaging in some make-believe with the shape (this leaf, a bird! that rock, a fish!). My mother-in-law (hardly an unobservant woman) doubted that she would have noticed in the rubble this stone that did indeed look like a heart and which, more than thirty years later, I still have.

Just like adults, children are likely to open up and meander through their emotions during a walk. Time and again, this happened when I went for walks with the children of Kittsville, the dance and cultural arts program I founded in Watts in the mid-1960s.

On Saturday mornings after a dance workout in a school auditorium, if I didn't have the kids over to my house in Beverly Hills for a swim, or take them on some other outing, often we'd troop down to the beach in Santa Monica.

We swam, we splashed in the waves, we built sand castles, and we walked in the sand to strengthen the legs and the thighs. We searched for shells, examined the designs, discussed the whys and wherefores of the Creators. We walked, walked, walked.

When it was time for lunch, we often sat down on the beach in a circle with the food the mothers had prepared, and we had spirited conversations. The children were so open then, so relaxed: they told me about school, their families, their habits, about how they felt about themselves.

I remember one little girl with a pretty face and nice manners who was so oversized. Because of her weight, she was not able to walk as quickly as everyone else in the group. When we found her lagging too far behind, we slowed down or walked back toward her so she wouldn't feel ugly. As we walked all together again, we kept praising her into wanting to get herself in shape, encouraging her to exercise more and eat foods that would help her. This child's participation in Kittsville had always been sporadic. When she did not come for a long while, I wondered if she had given up on herself. I was greatly relieved to find out sometime later that she had kept walking on her own more and more, and eating more and more of the kind of food that helped her help herself.

I witnessed the balm that walking can be during an engagement in Cape Town, South Africa, in the early 1970s.

As I love to watch the sunrise, particularly over water, when I was in Cape Town I couldn't wait to get to the beach every morning with my daughter, who was twelve at the time.

What a beautiful sight it was—the waves, the first light. How breathtaking, awe-inspiring—and such a contrast to the wicked premises and practices that dominated South Africa. The early-morning time spent at the beach was a refuge from all that was so ugly about that nation. So Kitt and I walked and ran, ran and walked, talked, looked. And one day we came upon this knot of children on the edge of the beach. The children were brown, black, white. Their assembly, of course, was illegal.

As Kitt and I drew closer to the children, we discovered that all or at least some of them had seen my photograph in the paper.

"Urta, Urta, Urta, Urta, Urta Kitt!"

I beckoned them to join us in our running and walking. They were wary about venturing from their spot, fearing that some authority might discover their interracial group and punish them. They all became more comfortable when I assured them that if they were with me, they had nothing to fear. (If they were hassled, I was more than ready to go to the press.)

Every day thereafter, the children joined my daughter and me at the beach. Day after day, the group grew larger as a friend told a friend who told a friend, thereby setting a principle and breaking a law that was stupid.

The children's running along the beach with the breeze, and at moments making a chant of my name—"Urta, Urta,

Urta, Urta, Urta Kitt!"—led to free and easy walking. As we walked, the children told me about their lives and how much they wanted apartheid eradicated. Talk about bolstering your faith in humanity! What wonderful exchanges my daughter and I had with these children: children with common sense that some grown-ups seem to lose.

Given all the benefits to be derived from something so natural to us *Homo sapiens,* it is unfortunate that so many of us walk very little *and* very badly.

I am reminded here of one of my people-watching moments in New York City as I sat in my car at a red light. Of all the people who passed my car, one man held my attention. This man, whom I took to be Chinese (dressed as he was in traditional Chinese folk garb), was not walking, but shuffling. I was reminded of the sights of Hong Kong: a long bamboo stick across the shoulder blades, at each end a huge bundle, both arms slung over the stick with the weight of the load forcing the feet to bounce and shuffle along. Without a load this man's body behaved as though the load were still there.

How we walk says a lot about our state of mind (depressed

people often walk with their heads down and their shoulders slumped). We can also read into people's walk their attitude toward their bodies, their training and experience.

Dancers usually walk with great outlook, their bodies at attention: back straight, toes turned out, center of the body forward, shoulders relaxed, stomach in, head level on the shoulders. Their steps are usually straight ahead, with the attitude "I have someplace to go!"

Basketball players often walk as if they want something to throw.

Manual laborers often walk as though they want to pick something up.

In various ways our walk says who we are. This tells me that if we improve the quantity and quality of our walking, we can improve the quantity and quality of our lives, with the attitude that "I have someplace to go!"

Imagine yourself in a bad mood, yet summoning the will to walk properly (and to breathe properly, too). The infusion of oxygen will clear the mind and energize the body, alleviating tension and extinguishing rage or fear of whatever plagues the spirit. With back straight and head up you might just catch sight of something beautiful or bizarre—something that takes your mind off your troubles. Something or someone interesting.

As walking is my number one exercise, I so often walk when I don't feel like it. Yes!—thank goodness for my dogs. Often after their morning or evening walk, if I have been feeling a bit out of sorts, I find that a walk soothes me. Sometimes, after walking the dogs, I am fueled to do more walking. I might then decide to walk this two-mile path near my house that takes me between thirty and forty minutes.

During walks near my home, I never fail to find something wonderful. On one particularly magnificent Sunday morning in the spring of 2000, a day very comfortable for walking, with the need for only a sweater, and with nature just coming into bloom, the wonderment was a group of elders rejuvenating themselves.

They all looked to be about my age. Up and down the hills and dales, across the brooks, and into the woods they went, this group of about twelve ladies led by a man much younger than they. Some of the women had staffs of fallen tree branches, and they all walked slowly, yet their spirits exuded vim.

Rejuvenate! (It's Never Too Late)

Some bent over to pet Aba and Mutzi, who are very much people lovers. I greeted the group as I passed by, cheering them, too: it's a rather heavy trek up and down the path they were on. It made me feel good that someone cared enough to take these ladies out for a walk, and on not so easy a trail.

If you are capable of putting one foot in front of the other, you should really take advantage of that ability. Be sure that when you do, you wear shoes that are fit for walking. If, like me, you can handle walking in ankle weights, don't leave home without them. Fit food is important, too. As with all my activities, I would not be able to manage the walking that I do if I did not feed myself foods—without being fanatical—that enable me to do, do, do (which I discuss in the chapter "Eat").

Walking a trail or down the street, through meals, conversations, decisions—when we can walk, we should. Doing so fortifies mind and body for those times when we truly need to pick up the pace or even break into a run. Indeed, the more we walk, the better we run.

Run is what I certainly had to do one morning in the spring of 2000 when one of my dogs suffered a brutal assault from three dogs in our neighborhood who somehow got onto my property despite the fencing. I had to rush to Aba's rescue, I had to get her to the hospital, I had to file a police report, I had to deal with my other dog, Mutzi, who was trembling so for the longest time. Plus, I had to get myself ready (physically and emotionally) to leave the house for the recording of *The Wild Party* cast album.

I had planned to spend the morning and afternoon writing and doo-daddling about. Instead I had to shift into emergency mode and *move, move, move!* Yes, I was hurrying and, yes, there were tears, but through it all I maintained a measure of calm and efficiency: no screaming or yelling, no ranting or raving. "Take deep breaths and cry later," I told myself.

Were it not for the persistent good caretaking—walking included!—of my body and mind, I might well have collapsed from the trauma. In the midst of this tragedy, I still found time to "walk." I walked around the lawn crying at one point, and when my daughter came over, we walked through the experience, talking about how we were feeling as we talked about what had happened. Walking through is talking through is breathing through an experience, bringing peace.

Peace and stamina for a day is all the more likely, I have found, when at the top of an especially full day, I walk through it: seeing the duties and desires on my schedule, seeing how I would like things to go, and preparing myself emotionally for foreseeable challenges and for the unexpected.

At the end of the day, I find that it helps to retrace my steps as I ready myself for bed.

"Eartha, what did you do today?"

And I think.

One night, I remembered watching two Canada geese as I ate a breakfast of two eggs, oatmeal, a piece of fish with sautéed onions and a slice of tomato, and a half slice of brown toast with olive oil. (I felt great all day.) Then, I saw myself walking the dogs (there went forty minutes) and then exercising at my kitchen counter: up and down in knee bends, stretching the thighs, and thanking the gods for the two geese and the constant visit of the cardinal.

I went through the rest of my day, including *The Wild Party* rehearsal, to the point where I was drifting off to sleep, comforted by the knowledge that I knew how I had spent the time, and that throughout the day I had taken good care of the tools the gods have given me.

Make a list of literal and figurative occasions for walking to which you would like to commit.

1. _____

2. _____

3. _____

4. _____

5. _____

6. _____

7. _____

8. _____

9. _____

10. _____

SEVEN

Balance

For me, nothing is better for balance than somersaults, which balance the inner-ear liquid. There's also standing upside down with your legs against a wall, holding the position for as long as you can (you may feel dizzy upon returning to a normal stance, but that's normal—at least for me). If you are not up to somersaults or handstands, try this: Stand on one foot while holding the other foot by the ankle and extending the free hand into the air. Try to hold the position for about thirty seconds, and then do the same with the other foot. Repeat twice. (If this exercise is a little unmanageable at first, hold on to something such as a wall or a chair, gradually moving away from the wall or chair when confidence is obtained.)

My life has been rich and long, I am convinced, in part because my life has been a balancing act: duties and desires in proper order, and an avoidance of extremes.

As much as I love my work, I have not let it overwhelm my life. You can be committed to your work without being married to the job to such an extent that you neglect family.

The plan may be to work, work, work, secure the home front, and then devote time to family. Sadly, all too often things do not work out that way. The work, work, work goes on and on, and the next thing you know, the children are off to college or getting married. There you are a middle-aged burnout with dim memories of your children's stages and phases of growth. You may even be perplexed as to why it is that your now grown children want little to do with you or rarely think that you need them.

I certainly understand that circumstances force some people to work long hours, five or six days a week. But many among us work, work, work out of vanity, ego, and money madness. If family time must be sacrificed, it ought to be out of need, not greed.

No matter what compels a person to spend a great deal of time working, one can make time for family if one is creative.

I traveled with my daughter from the time the doctor said I could (once her immune system was strong enough to ward off diseases). Kitt was about three months old and I had a three-month engagement at the Talk of the Town; so off to London Kitt and I went. I knew it would be ridiculous to try to be Supermom, so I hired a nanny. The nanny was not a surrogate mother, however. Kitt was with me, for example, during show time, in my dressing room, so that during every moment of freedom I had, I could mother her: hold her, change her nappies, feed her, massage her legs (because she was born with her knees turned in)—anything to have that mommy contact.

Balancing motherhood and work was taxing. When fatigue got me too stressed, I would take a time-out: standing on my head with my legs against a wall for a few minutes, relieving the fatigue by boosting the circulation. I accomplished the same by getting down on the floor and rolling, rolling, rolling over and over and over.

I balanced my need for exercise and my need to play with my child by coming up with things that would simultaneously satisfy both needs. There was Reeda-Reeda-Ronka, where I lay on my back and balanced little Kitt on my legs, pulling her up and down, in and out. Kitt had fun riding my legs, while Mommy strengthened her legs and stomach muscles. The laughter we shared playing Reeda-Reeda-Ronka was another form of exercise: a massage of the spirit for us two.

I was a sad Mommy when Kitt became too long-legged for Reeda-Reeda-Ronka. Soon, she became too big for our other little games. When she was about twelve, I began to feel that empty nest coming on, realizing that she would want to spend more and more time with her friends and that the boys would soon be coming around. How did I balance this new ism in my life? By finding something to do when I was not working.

Because I had spent time with my child, when she left the nest I had that spiritual "massage" of great memories from the times we had shared. Our bedtime storytime, for instance. It was not always the usual affair. Often, instead of reading Kitt a story, I had her tell me a story that would really work her brain. As I lay beside her in her bed, she created a story around everything that she saw on the ceiling and the walls of her room, beginning at one corner and coming full circle. Every shadow, crack, nook, et cetera. She had to do this without lapsing into "and uh . . ." when she could not come up quick with a plausible story element. Oh, yes, the story had to be logical and it had to flow. Kitt was smart: when she could not make the story flow, she'd start laughing and I'd start laughing—but she'd have to start the story all over again. I believe that this is one of the reasons that today my daughter has a keen, rapid mind. What a marvelous way our special storytime combined fun and training.

I was able to balance work and motherhood quite well because of the nature of my work: Kitt could go with me wherever in the world I had a job, and always there was real togetherness. When, for instance, we lived in Los Angeles, and I was engaged at the Plaza Hotel's Persian Room, Kitt was in New York with me, and we enjoyed walks in Central Park every morning and on Sundays. When a day did not permit a real outing, we sometimes had picnics in the suite: bedsheets and towels were our blankets; we ordered up food from the hotel or from a nearby restaurant.

Many do not have jobs that are child-friendly. I am convinced that there would be a lot more balance in families if workplaces had day care centers, so that during a coffee break and at lunchtime, parents could spend time with their children: children would get small doses of the nurturing they need; parents would not have to wait until early morning, late at night, and the weekend to satisfy their need to nurture. This would free up parents from guilt about leaving the care of their children to others for eight or more hours every day. Life would be more integrated for the worker, and that would benefit the employer. (I never will forget that photograph of John F. Kennedy Jr. under his father's desk. And I cheer those parents who have found a way to earn a living from their homes, even though it may mean less income than were they working outside the home.)

Even if you do not have children, you ought to be reasonable about work. There are other relationships at stake: friends, amours, parents. There's the need for play as well.

If you are consumed by your work, you may neglect your health—eating on the run, eating junk food, eating without being aware of how much you have already eaten, and eating nonvaluable calories. (When on the go, carry along a bag of nuts, fruit, cheese, and veggie sticks.)

"Balanced meals." You have probably been hearing that since you were knee-high to a grasshopper. If you are not already on solid ground here, you'd do well to make "balanced meals" your mantra. Say it to yourself over and over—balanced meals, balanced meals, balanced meals. (You will get a taste of what is, for me, a balanced diet in the next chapter.)

It is not only keeping the nose to the grindstone that keeps many people from eating a balanced diet. For many, especially women, the problem is more concern for having the good figure than having good health.

I had a girlfriend in London who made this mistake. My

friend was an attractive woman: blond, blue-eyed, great figure. One of the many times that I was working in London, she took me to lunch almost every day. It was always at a ritzy restaurant where she knew her husband (a wealthy man) would be lunching.

Lunch with my pretty friend was not a pretty sight. She popped some pills, had a martini, and when the lunch of salad and a protein came (usually that was it, and the same for me), she ate little, as she watched her husband out of the corner of her eye. What was that about? Another woman? Hardly. Her husband was always eating with a group of men, talking business it seemed to me.

Her husband was a jolly soul. The first time we were introduced was at this restaurant. On his way to wherever, he stopped to greet us at our table. After the introductions were made, he mentioned that he had seen me running the six-mile path in the park along Piccadilly (about a block from the Mayfair Hotel, where I was staying).

"I do that also every morning," he said. "I have to work it off, because I love my food and drink too much." My friend's husband had found a way to balance his appetites, his body's needs, and his business.

I knew he wasn't really talking to me when he said, "If you love food and drink, exercise is better than pills."

After this lunch, my friend and I walked along Brompton Road looking at the interesting antiques in the shop windows.

"I hate exercise!" she exclaimed out of nowhere. "I've tried."

"For a short time, to lose weight, I tried pills, too, only to find out that this quick fix made me irritable." I told her that experience had taught me how important it is to be sane about losing weight, and to stick to what is natural for me.

Pills that made her irritable, too much alcohol, and too little food—she looked great, but what a mess she was. I didn't want to think about what her insides looked like. While looking great on the outside, she was deteriorating. In contrast, her husband was getting stronger and more distinguished-looking in his graying fifties. And he was enjoying his life. Fearing that she was losing him, she tried to hold on to him with all the wrong tools. Their relationship was obviously unbalanced. She cared more about possessing him than loving him or herself. If ever they'd had good communication, it had long since broken down.

My friend had imbalance in other areas of her life. Her

daughter was in a boarding school, so my friend had little to do when it came to being a mother. Plus, she had servants for everything. She spent her time lunching with friends and shopping, shopping, shopping. All play, no work: what a recipe for a wretched existence that can be.

People who, by reason of inheritance or marriage, do not have to work for their daily bread and who think that the world is nothing but a playground are as unbalanced as those who overwork. Too much play can lead to weakness and dissipation. Look at what happens to children who are never required to do any chores, who are given free rein to play, play, play, and who are given every single toy they ask for—spoiled brats. Ladies and gentlemen of excessive leisure spoil themselves in more ways than one. There is nothing wrong with not having to work, but I think that it is unhealthy to not spend some of your time in productive pursuits.

Of course, it is not only the rich who can be pathetically idle. People with able bodies and sound minds who prefer public assistance to work are off the beam as well. To ask for a helping hand when you hit a rough spot is one thing (and not a bad thing); choosing to spend your life on handouts when you could fend for yourself shrinks your potential, zaps your gumption, and you can end up really pitiful. It is so energizing (though it be a struggle at times) to do for yourself. (What a good example it sets for the children.) The more one is willing to do for oneself, the more likely it is that others will give that helping hand gladly.

Sorrow and joy—another place where balance is needed. The older we get, the more we deal with the deaths of loved ones. I do not feel that a death should be treated as a sad, sad, *sad* affair, with crying, crying, *crying,* moaning, moaning, *moaning,* being depressed and wearing yards of black forever. As I mentioned in the first chapter, I think that mourning is necessary, but if sorrow runneth over for too long, you can lose your wits (and your wit). I have been able to survive the deaths of people dear to me by balancing the mourning with celebrations of their lives.

At the news of a friend's death, I let the tears flow, but it's never long before there is a smile on my face, a smile that often expands into laughter.

When my friend from *New Faces of 1952* Ronny Graham died, I remembered how practically all of his life, Ronny had lived out of a suitcase (a small suitcase at that). He only made enough money in one job to last until another job came along, and sometimes debts mounted when there was a gap. But Ronny, ever the gentleman, never complained about anything that I could remember. He even laughed about his alimony payments. Remembering his laughter, his offstage antics, and the whole great fun we had doing the show brought a natural end to the tears.

It was the same when the call came of the death of Ronny's understudy in *New Faces,* Jimmie Komack, who had eventually become a producer for television shows, among them *Chico and the Man* and *Welcome Back, Kotter.* Oh, how I mourned Jimmie's absence from the planet. Then up popped the memories of Jimmie, and I was in stitches, particularly over the night he escorted me home after the *New Faces* opening-night party.

Jimmie was standing in my bedroom doorway when, after kicking off my high-heel shoes, I fell back on the bed and sighed, "I'm bushed!"

"Oh," said Jimmie, "I didn't know you were that way."

I was too tired to follow his train of thought and didn't realize what a misunderstanding there had been until some months later, when Jimmie called me after reading in a newspaper that I had a wealthy boyfriend.

"I see you have a boyfriend."

"Why shouldn't I have a boyfriend?"

"You told me you were butch."

"When did I tell you such a thing?" I was laughing by then.

"The night I took you home. When you fell back on the bed, you said, 'I'm butch.'"

I broke out into hysterics at that point. "Bushed, Jimmie, *bushed.*" I laughed even more.

Ronny, Jimmie, others—every time someone I cherished died, if feelings of joy did not arise spontaneously, I have had the presence of mind to talk to myself: "Eartha, remember the good times, remember the fun. Remember."

I could live another life on memories of the fun I have had with friends—and what a wonderful range of friends I have had over the years: heads of state, heads of companies, teachers, a horticulturist. (What is the saying about horticulturists? You can lead a whore to culture, but you can't make her think?) Anyway, my point here is that friendships outside of the entertainment world (as well as in it) have enriched me so.

When fame came, I never felt the need to associate solely with the rich and famous. I have never cultivated friendships for the sake of being able to name-drop or to piggyback on the prestige and privileges of others. "My kind of people" are people who are thinkers—and fun. They leave behind as much as they take away.

Having a balance of friends has meant that I have moved and breathed and had my being in a wide world. I could go from the Aga Khan's yacht party to my housekeeper's get-together without missing a beat and being discombobulated. The range has kept me fit to be a true citizen of the world.

Speaking of fitness . . .

A balanced attitude toward physical fitness is crucial. Have you just made a resolution to shape up? If so—bravo! But, please, oh, please, do not go overboard, thinking that you can make up for lost time. You can hurt yourself that way. When beginning an exercise regimen, it is imperative that the workout be well suited for you and that you increase *gradually* the number of sets of an exercise or the number of miles you bike (or walk or run) or the poundage of the weights you lift or wear on your ankles and wrists (which I do). Sure and steady increase in ability brings exquisite satisfaction, especially when you stay with it.

An obsession with exercise can result in a "perfect" body, but it can also leave you off-balance in other areas of your life. Are you devoting so much time to exercise that you're not reading, not taking care of your home, not attending to your relationships?

A balance between work and play, between work and family, balance in friendships, balanced meals, balanced exercise—everywhere balance, balance, balance if you want to keep your spirit fit, and your life from becoming ramshackle. (I am reminded here of the many great after-surgery faces that I have seen atop neglected bodies.)

Above all, have a balanced perspective on yourself.

I never wanted to be a star at any cost (never really wanted to be a star at all). My ambition (if you want to call it that) has been to use well the tools that I have been given. Eartha Kitt did not want to be like someone else, but to be the me that I am, to fulfill the me that the gods intended.

I resisted the craving to be the top-top, hottest-hottest superstar. Every step of the way, yes, I have reached. I have

never, however, seen my career as a ladder and myself straining to get to the top rung. My career has been a wonderful
walk, not a climb. If I am on some ladder of success, maybe
even a rung away from the top, I'm not so sure I want to set
foot on that very last rung. I prefer to leave the world with the
foot poised in the air. That way I'll always feel I have someplace to go if I so choose.

If ever I lapsed into a moment of perverse ambition, I managed a reality check: taking a good look at my life and
acknowledging my good fortune.

The kick I get out of doing housework is not just the kick of
the exercise. Doing housework is also one of the ways that I
maintain the proper quotient of humility. When I am taking
care of my home, whether it's oiling a piece of furniture,
rehanging a painting, or cleaning my toilet bowl, I can truly
see what I have been able to achieve.

When I look around at what I have and remember whence
I came—I bow down and say thank you: thank you . . . the
Creators, whoever you are; thank you . . . my ancestors, whoever you are; thank you . . . friends who have been true
friends; thank you . . . the spirits of the wonderful lovers I
have known; thank you . . . Mrs. Bishop and Mrs. Mearson

and Mrs. Banks, the schoolteachers whom I will never forget because they helped the unwanted ugly duckling Eartha Mae to have confidence in herself and to become something, if not a swan.

Moments like these keep me from taking myself too seriously. And so, I stay balanced in my soul and thus clear about the necessity of balance in every facet of my life—not being fanatical, but using common sense.

Make note of the areas in your life where there is unbalance.

1. _____

2. _____

3. _____

4. _____

5. _____

6. _____

7. _____

8. _____

9. _____

10. _____

EIGHT

Eat

Eat to nourish the mind and body, not only to be pleasured.

Let the midday meal be your largest meal of the day, not dinner. Drink a glass of water before a meal (at a restaurant, forgo the bread and butter—or at least eat less of it, or eat the salad first). Drink a glass of water after a meal to aid the digestion.

After a meal, walk if you can—even if it is only around in circles in your home. Whatever you do, try not to go to sleep for at least three hours after dinner.

I love food. More than that, I have a great respect for food. The seed of this esteem? With a name like Eartha, one is given to think about the source of most of what we eat, the earth.

Nothing will guarantee an abundance of tomorrows; however, you definitely increase the likelihood of having many, many upbeat days on earth if you eat intelligently. My relationship to food has had an enormous impact on my well-being and so, on my entire life.

I still savor many long-ago meals in various countries, as I do the sheer experience of having tasted cuisines of an array of cultures. The French Moroccan is one of my favorite cuisines—the combinations of vegetables and the couscous and the protein (chicken, lamb, veal). On this, I could really pig out, as the saying goes.

There's the best Chinese meal I have ever had, from the kitchen of Mr. Kwong in Burma. I had done a benefit for a school there; as a thank-you, Mr. Kwong, allegedly the fourth-richest Chinese man in the world, had me to his home for dinner. Just his family, two friends, and me.

The house was delicious. The artwork made it a warm, friendly museum, and the whole house was teakwood, the hardest wood in the world. Every piece of furniture—different shades of teakwood. Even the bathhouse at the pool was teak.

Teakwood, too, was the lazy Susan bearing so many different dishes and huge bowls of rice—plain rice. Delicate beef dishes, shrimp dishes, fish dishes, and wonderful vegetable dishes—with one touch to the lazy Susan, you could partake of whatever you desired at the moment. It was so easy to desire a lot, because everything was cooked with great simplicity—just enough to bring out the flavor. I could have eaten all night and not gained an ounce, I felt.

I could go on and on about fantastic meals I have eaten over the years. Gourmet this and gourmet that, delicacies A to Z. I have always been willing to try just about anything. The smorgasbord of cuisines I have known has never, however, lured me away from the food I like best.

Basically, it is peasant food, the food eaten by the folk closest to the good earth.

For me, a good breakfast might be Irish oatmeal (coarse, unfancified) with about two tablespoons of nonfat yogurt. (If I want it sweet, I add a little honey.) Along with this, I eat the whites of two boiled eggs, the yolk of one (the other yolk goes to my dogs), and a slice of dark toast topped with about two tablespoons of olive oil, a large slice of onion, and two slices of tomato. Along with this, I often have a banana. A glass of milk is usually the beverage, but often all I have is a glass of water or perhaps a cup of green tea. I have found that a good strong cup of coffee can lift me when such is needed.

Lunch is typically a piece of chicken or fish (cooked any style), and a green salad with a low-fat cheese and dressed with a mustard, olive oil, and vinegar mix. (One of my favorite salads is feta cheese–broccoli.)

Once a week, lunch might be a rare hamburger, topped with lots of raw onions and a few slices of tomato and sandwiched by leaves of romaine lettuce instead of bread. (If I'm in the mood for bread, it's always a dark bread.) On the side, pickles and cabbage slaw—very filling. After such a lunch, it is rare that I have a desire for an afternoon snack. If I do, some melon, pineapple, mango, orange, grapefruit, papaya, or other fruit will usually suffice.

My dinner is always much lighter than my lunch, and I hardly ever eat late at night, as I know that the body will not burn off the food as it does during the day when I am out and about and doing things. (If work is such that I am not able to eat until late at night, I satisfy my hunger with a bowl of oatmeal or a little yogurt and melon or banana.)

A typical dinner for me is a piece of fish (sautéed or steamed with lots of onions and garlic or fried with cornmeal and olive oil) along with some kind of green vegetable (collard greens and steamed spinach are favorites). I might also have a baked sweet potato or baked Irish potato (skin and all).

Another favored dish is rice and black beans. The time I spent, as a young adult, with New York City Cubans and Puerto Ricans sparked my love for this dish (not knowing then that beans are an excellent combination of protein and carbohydrates). I recall, too, a marvelous dish I had in Nigeria: a mix of rice and beans, chicken, grated coconut, banana, mango, and peanuts. (When I visited the sick in the hospitals there, I discovered that rice and beans was what most patients were served.)

I do not require heavy seasoning. Here and there I might toss in some fresh herbs or a dash or two of salt and pepper. Most of the seasoning I do is with an abundance of garlic and onion, which I have known to be healing foods since I was a child. (Also, I *love* all sorts of peppers.)

When I sit to table—breakfast, lunch, dinner—I am grateful: grateful that I was able to earn the money for the food, that I am able to prepare the food, and that I am physically able. Often, I think about the vitamins and minerals the foods supply, such as the calcium in the collards and the enzymes in mango, pineapple, and papaya.

I am grateful to have learned the value of simple foods: simple ingredients, simple to prepare, simply wonderful for my total well-being, and simply *not* overcooked.

Simplicity means that if there's a yen for a little sugar, I use honey (or occasionally, raw sugar). If rice, brown rice, usually. Simple as in "unsophisticated" versus the refined foods that Queen Victoria made all the rage in her purification campaign, elevating white over dark, and therefore white bread, white sugar, white flour, white rice—so much of the nutrients gone.

I have found that my eating is all the more nourishing an experience if the environment is beautiful. This is not achieved solely through expensive dinnerware and other table paraphernalia. Clean is beautiful. A little two-dollar plant is beautiful. (Whatever you find beautiful is beautiful!) Another thing: I try not to break bread with people of negative energy. An unpleasant tablemate spoils a meal and can bring hazard to the digestion.

It may seem as if I have a lot of rules when it comes to eating. Actually, I have not rules but guidelines. I have never been fanatical about anything. The same applies to my eating. To be superstrict would take a lot of energy and box me in. Remember: eating should be to nourish as well as to pleasure.

At times, some things are more important than watching what I eat: things such as cordiality and community. So when I am doing a play and there's a backstage celebration (a cast member's birthday perhaps) that includes a too-rich-for-me cake, I partake of the cake (if I like the person). Participating in the celebration is warming and the loving thing to do (and I know that having a few bites of the cake is not going to kill me).

Similarly, if I happen to be at someone's home for dinner and the menu includes collard greens cooked with fatback or ham hocks, I don't turn up my nose and screech, "How can you eat that!" As with the rich birthday cake, I eat the greens (but not the fatback or the fat from the hocks).

Likewise, I do not aggravate myself after an occasional indulgence of my own creation, such as the time during the winter holidays that I ordered two tins of pecans from a specialty shop: one for myself, the other a gift for a friend, who never got hers. Now and then I have a Snickers bar. But, of course, as George Washington Carver said, the peanut (like his beloved yam) is a miracle food. For one, they clean the colon, and roughage is good for the soul as well as the body.

I must say, even my indulgences are simple, nuts mostly. Those who think I have had countless caviar and champagne days are sorely mistaken. Yes, I have (and still do) adored beluga and Dom Pérignon, but I learned years ago the harm that could come from having too much of these good things, or anything.

Along with simplicity, the health of the food is extremely important to me: as fresh as possible and as pure as possible for optimum nutrition. This is why I have always tried to grow my own food no matter where I was living. I have even grown herbs and tomatoes on the windowsills of my dressing room when there was southern exposure.

I did my best and largest growing on the property of about three acres that I bought in Beverly Hills in 1957. There, I had a tremendous garden, and it was my pride. Tomatoes, collard greens, cabbage, squash, scallions, onions, zucchini, comfrey, string beans, carrots, beets—anything that would grow in that climate—and, oh, yes, okra. Naturally, I had fruit trees: orange, lemon, loquat, kumquat, and the only custard apple tree in Beverly Hills. I even planted seven avocado trees that took seven years to bear fruit, and the wait was worth it. I had lettuces of all kinds, with iron-rich romaine the most plentiful.

There was a big birdcage that I started with two white doves and two brown doves, which yielded thirty-four doves, all brown (I believe in integrating everything). I also had five hens and one rooster (a rooster needs five hens—don't ask why). We only ate the eggs, as everything around me becomes a pet.

Eating everything straight from the ground, clean and fresh, no pesticides—paradise! Such a benefit to my health, and, of course, to that of my daughter, who was about four or five years old when she started picking her own veggies for her meals. She even had a little wagon that she sometimes filled with her harvest and then stationed in the driveway with a sign—selling her wares.

That garden was a wonderworld for my daughter and me, as we tended it together—digging, hoeing, picking, tasting, watering—making good use of the good earth, toiling for our table, getting great exercise, having togetherness and bonding.

One day Kitt asked, "Mommy, if I keep digging, what will I find?"

I jokingly said, "China."

Knowing she was too young to understand the joke, I laughed at the situation, because for the longest time Kitt was digging in that same place looking for something called China.

Today, I have similar fun when my grandchildren come over and help me plant or harvest from my garden—tomatoes, zucchini, collards, comfrey, string beans, whatever. And when I see my harvest, I can feel the nourishment. The thought of it feeds the spirit and soul.

When growing my own food was not possible, whether in

America or abroad, to the extent possible I shopped for food daily at a market that carried healthy food.

Such marketing carries the bonus of getting acquainted with others, making friends, getting recipes and meal ideas. (People who care about quality food are usually sharers.) Curiosity about different kinds of foods exercises the mind, as do watching people's personalities and actions (how they examine the food) and wondering what meals people might be preparing based on what is in their basket or cart. Marketing for meals on a daily basis also means the body gets exercise.

I realize that not everyone can go to market daily. Still, I say, *make it possible*—at least once a week instead of once in a great while. The point here is to minimize the amount of quick-to-fix foods. The canned, frozen, boil-it-in-a-bag, and microwavable are convenient, I know; however, I think we pay a price for this convenience—less nutrients and more of what the body and mind do not need and what may even be harmful. When you are doing things quickly when it comes to feeding yourself, I think you are asking for a quicker passage through life, or perhaps a sickly passage. Make the time, take the extra step, like a woman I know who has two markets in walking distance. One market, with usually so-so fare, is about six blocks from her home; the other, which offers a wider selection and a better quality of fruits, vegetables, and fish, is a little less than a mile away. She has trained herself to go just about every day to the far market. It has become something of a ritual, one that does quadruple duty: she gets better food, a nice walk, and breathing-room time, and she saves on bus fare.

Simple food. Healthy food. This is my recipe.

And not too much food, either.

As a child, I never knew what it was to have an abundance of food. The people to whom I was given were poor. Moreover, I was the despised yella gal, good for nothing, according to them, except when there was work to be done.

So at an early age, I learned to make do. I became accustomed to surviving on a little bit, and on this little bit I was a hardy worker. I was never even allowed plenty for Sunday dinner, the big meal of the week. There was even less food when the preacher came to Sunday dinner. That man had no shame. He knew he was not in a house of plenty, yet he ate, ate, ate—huge first helping, seconds, thirds. On those Sundays or on any other day of the week I did not dare utter the words of Oliver Twist: "More, please."

What little I was given was, generally, quite good for the body because it was fresh and natural: collard greens, sweet potatoes, chicken, catfish, butterfish, grits, corn bread. It is true that fatback was often in the mix, and the fish and poultry were often deep-fried—and fried with lard; however, the fat would be burned with the cotton picking and other labor I had to do. (Besides, I never had that much to eat.)

Some people who never had a lot of food as children become gluttons. Such was not the case with me, as a consequence of the lean years to come and my career.

When I was a scholarship student in ballet school, I received a stipend of $10 a week. Five dollars went for the room I shared with one of the Dunham dancers (having moved out of my aunt's because I couldn't bear the feeling of being "in the way"). That left $5 for everything else, from food to transportation (five cents each way for the subway or bus).

Breakfast was a slice of pound cake and a glass of milk—five cents for the cake, five cents for the milk. After my ten o'clock dance class, and eleven-thirty technique class, I was ready for some lunch—five cents for a hot dog with lots and lots of mustard and onions and five cents for milk or coffee with milk. As for dinner—whatever, perhaps a hamburger (ten cents) with lots of mustard and onions, and water, water, water. (I was never interested in soda pop, other than to redeem the bottles and buy with the penny a chocolate bar with peanuts.)

This was the way it was most days until we had a real show that paid $45 per week. After union dues, the cost of makeup, et cetera, life was a bit higher on the hog. Still, there was no abundance of anything.

But I learned that living frugally can be rewarding in terms of the health of the body. (Clutter can enslave you: the more you have, the more you have to be responsible for.) I could not afford much, so I ate little. I ate what I needed to eat to keep the body strong and the mind alert (a salad and the protein from chicken and fish). I became aware of what foods gave me energy that lasted and what foods gave a quick high and a rapid downer. (The common pound cake and hot dogs of my youth were, I think, far healthier than they are today.)

Even if someone treated me to a meal, as a dancer and as someone whose body was much admired, I had great incentive not to overeat. Too, in the early days, I did not want to be a problem when it came to the fit of whatever costume was handed down to me. (That sense of never wanting to be a problem also meant I often wore shoes that were too small. Yes, I managed, but, boy, did I pay for it later in life.)

Making do on a little bit of food continued during my early days in Paris as a solo artist.

Most days I made do with lots and lots of water and the *petit déjeuner* that came with my hotel room, which cost seven hundred francs a day, which often I could not pay for months at a time. (At that time, three hundred and fifty francs equaled one American dollar.) This breakfast consisted of two large croissant-confitures, a large café au lait, and a slab of sweet butter. After breakfast, to burn, burn, burn the fat of the bread and jam and butter, I spent the rest of the morning exercising on the balcony looking at the Champs-Élysées with the feeling that something wonderful was going to happen.

What a blessing it was when someone treated me to a meal, such as the time a boyfriend took me to an expensive restaurant for dinner. As we ate our salads, we were tasting the steak yet to arrive, because this restaurant had a reputation for great steaks.

With great pride, the waiter placed the popular steaks before us. Then came the sauce.

That sauce lay before me like a million calories to my eyes. Being always conscious of body fat, I said, "No sauce, please."

Heads turned. The whole world stood still. The waiter walked away in a huff.

Soon, a voice came from the walls behind me. As it got closer and closer to my ears, I understood the voice to be that of the chef. Soon, there he was before me in full chef regalia. Obviously, the waiter had told Monsieur Le Chef that I had refused his sauce.

I sat there, stiff as a board, feeling like that South Carolina yella gal, a problem.

"Je ne fais pas la sauce pour le steak, mais le steak pour la sauce!" screamed Monsieur Le Chef.

What a concept, I thought: the steak for the sauce, not the sauce for the steak?

Out of embarrassment and respect for this popular, celebrated chef, I discreetly put the sauce on my beautiful steak, with Monsieur Le Chef "helping" me by the spoonful. *"Un, deux, trois, quatre—suffit!"*

Yes, indeed, *enough!*

Rejuvenate! (It's Never Too Late)

"Alors, maintenant, goûte!"

As I obliged the command to "taste!" I counted the calories in each bite mentally—*un, deux, trois . . . mille*—and I swear I could feel the fat edging on me with every morsel.

The taste of this rich-rich, popular sauce was fantastic; however, the body went into shock, so unaccustomed was it to this much richness. Then my boyfriend *had* to order cheese and fruit, and then he *had* to order flan, and for the finish, a cordial. The sauce notwithstanding, I enjoyed the experience, aware that I might never have a chance like this again.

Certainly, I needed the walking that my boyfriend and I did after the meal, looking at the beauty of Paris, her lights, her charm—all the while that I analyzed how my beautiful steak sauce affected me. I thanked the gods that the portions had been small and that there had been a salad and *haricots verts.* After that meal, for me—definitely no sauces, except on special occasions. Or if a master chef is looking over my shoulder.

One of the many things I love about Europe is the tradition of sane portions: just enough to satisfy, not enough to leave one horribly bloated, heavy, and lethargic. It really is unfortunate that large portions seem to be the American way, with food, generally, piled so high on a plate that one feels it must all be eaten. Consider how we often brag more about how much food is served in a particular restaurant than about how well the food tastes. (Advice: When in a restaurant that offers outsize portions, order children's portions. If you are a party of two, choose a meal you both can enjoy and share—one order, two plates. Even if there is a charge for sharing, it is a small price to pay to keep yourself from overeating.)

When I had the money to eat whatever and however much I wanted, I couldn't break the habit of making do on a little. Growing up with food so scarce, I also became almost obsessive about never, ever wasting food. The sense of never knowing when the next meal would be stayed with me. That keeps me from leaving food on the plate when dining out. I have never been ashamed of the doggie bag. ("I never go anywhere without my Tupperware!") From an airplane to the finest restaurant, if there are decent leftovers, I take them along when I leave, for tomorrow or for my dogs. If there are leftovers from my table at home—to the dogs or to the compost or into the refrigerator or freezer. (And whatever happened to pot liquor? At Chez Eartha, these juices from a pot of vegetables do not go down the drain. As in the "olden days" I consume it, either drinking it up or saving it to flavor a future pot. Waste not, want not.)

Oddly enough, I can sometimes go for long periods without eating anything. The next thing I know, Eartha is irritable. And the mind asks, "When's the last time you've eaten?" Oops! And I go eat.

I urge you to really think about how much you eat. If you tend to overeat, you were probably *trained* to do so. Perhaps when you eat, you hear your mother commanding, "Eat *everything* on your plate!" and perhaps that plate held enough for two. If you are obsessed with getting your "money's worth" at a restaurant, understand that this can result in your getting much more than you bargained for.

Listen to your body. When the stomach says, "I'm full!"— stop! Put the fork down! Put the food in the refrigerator! Eat only what you really need. Learn to make do with a little. Don't be like that uncaring, unsharing preacher who came to Sunday dinner. Even today the thought of him is an appetite suppressant, as is a meal I had in Stuttgart, when Orson Welles and I were there doing *Faust*. It was one of the most outrageous meals I have ever had.

Our hosts were an American couple, living in Germany because the husband was in the army. I had made their acquaintance when they came to see the show, and when they invited me (and the whole cast) to come to brunch one Sunday, I thought how sweet, what a charm.

And what a spread. Talk about soups to nuts: grits, bacon and eggs, biscuits, waffles with melted butter, jam, jelly, corn bread, macaroni and cheese, collard greens and cabbage cooked with fatback and ham hocks, sweet potato pie, coconut pie, candied sweet potatoes, potato salad, black-eyed peas with ham hocks, string beans with fatback, spareribs, mixed salad with a mayonnaise-based dressing, apple pie. The Mr. and Mrs. were African-Americans. The lady of the house wanted to please me with home cooking Southern-style, which I greatly appreciated.

There was so much food that I was full before I had a morsel of anything. I had a taste of everything out of politeness: I knew how much effort had gone into this meal and how much the lady of the house wanted to please with a welcome table. With so much to taste, I ended up eating too much. I did not want to eat for days afterward.

When I look back on the scene, I remember that the Mrs.

was completely out of shape. Her husband, however, was in great shape, eating all this Southern-style home cooking with beer or Scotch to boot, and anything else he wanted. But, being a soldier, he worked out daily. On the other hand, his wife, who went above and beyond when it came to satisfying his appetites, was not taking care of herself. (Yes, ladies, the way to a man's heart may be through his stomach, as we are told, but it should not be through yours.)

And how do I feel about diets? I say, beware.

It has been proven that diets do not last and can be dangerous, too. I have watched people around me go with the fad—even to the extreme of having only liquid for a week—and then find themselves so weak that the slightest movement leads to exhaustion and momentary loss of memory. In Paris, I knew of models who ate cotton soaked in olive oil. It was only a matter of time before they went on an eating binge.

Sensible food and sane portions combined with exercise—simplicity, simplicity, simplicity. Nothing extreme. This is what I have always recommended to anyone who sought my counsel on shedding pounds. "Eat less, walk more—and breathe!"—that's how I have summed it up. I have also advised some against wanting to shed too many pounds, urging them to seek the weight appropriate for their bodies instead of striving to be superthin.

We cannot all look like models and should not have that desire. I love fashion. It is a great and wonderful business (but I don't want it to make me feel guilty if I don't keep up with it). It drives me mad, however, when the runway models all look like sticks in clothes that only they can wear, with designers giving the impression that a style is for everyone— just as some think that diets can be one-size-fits-all.

Deprivation is as harmful as overindulging.

There is certainly a lot to choose from when it comes to an eating regimen. No carbohydrates. High protein. No fat. Low fat. No red meat. Vegan. Vegetarian. Superhigh fiber. All raw. One day nuts are good for you, and the next day they're on the no-no list. One day we're told that eggs are hazards, the next day—*bon appétit!* A person can end up frustrated following the fads and pursuing extremes.

Consulting a physician or nutritionist about what you should or should not eat might be a good thing. Whether or not you seek expert advice, you owe it to yourself to do your homework: Notice how different foods (and various quantities) affect your body, your mood, your mind. Acquire a curiosity about what different foods provide (or do not provide).

We need to eat, because we need to nourish ourselves, and we ought to delight in the earth's offerings. So, eat! No more than your mind and body can handle and no less than they need.

EARTHA KITT

Begin a list of changes in your diet that you know are long overdue.

1. _____
2. _____
3. _____
4. _____
5. _____
6. _____
7. _____
8. _____
9. _____
10. _____

NINE

Etceterate

I do not live by breathing, stretching, bending, rocking-and-rolling, releasing, walking, balancing, and eating properly alone. I do many other things to make the most of my mind and body, and of my years. Perhaps you will find things you can use in the following potpourri.

Rise and Shine!

I exercise, usually, the minute I wake up. The covers are thrown back and the legs go up into the air: kicking, kicking, kicking. Then, I lean over to touch my toes. My stomach is tight after breathing in and breathing out (slowly), followed by isometric breathing (panting like a dog). I do this bed exercise because I never want to take that first step into the day feeling stiff. The stiffer the body, the less you are going to do. Morning aches can often be done away with by warming up and/or getting into a hot bath. I do both usually.

Bathe

Showers are popular, but I prefer a bath in the morning and before bed. Sitting in the warm water gets my muscles ready for my more intensive morning exercises (from walking my dogs to the aerobics class at a center near my home).

A bath before bed relaxes my mind and body, enhancing my chance of a good night's rest. Usually, the only thing I put into my bath is baby oil. Occasionally, if I'm aching, I add Epsom salt, and sometimes, I am in the mood for a bubble bath.

Now and then, at night, I'll have a few candles going in the bathroom. I really do not need a lot of props to get me into the mood for the soothing that a bath offers; however, I like the romantic feeling of candles, even though, yes, I'm alone (believe it or not). Further conducive to relaxation is the view from my bathroom window. I can behold a vast amount of nature, chamomile tea for the eyes (and the eyes are the window to the soul, they say).

My bath is not done until, after patting my body dry, I apply baby oil or lotion. (Whenever I get out of water, I moisturize every inch of my skin.)

Face It

You do not need a lot of expensive potions to take care of your face. I feel that the best skin care is keeping the insides clean by keeping to healthy eating. Exercise can also give your face a lift, as can fresh air and a moisturizer. Fundamental, too, is keeping the face clean. I have always used baby oil to clean off my makeup, followed by a light buffing with a soft loofah pad. I wash my face with fresh lemon sometimes.

I do not crave facials. It is true that a facial is relaxing; however, after a facial I have never looked any younger. (I might have felt younger, though; but any kind of exercise can do that.)

Get Naked

I have a full-length mirror on the door of a closet in my bedroom. I look at my whole self in this mirror in the morning and at night before I go to bed. This is not narcissism, but rather a desire to assess myself for the sake of taking care. With a good look in the mirror—"Oh, what do I have to work on here?"—I can see, for instance, whether I have reached that extra five pounds, the point at which I know I have to take action. And, yes, it does encourage me to keep taking care of myself when I see how well I have done, and I get annoyed when I see that I have not.

Don't be ashamed of your body. If there are areas that need improvement, how can you work on them if you do not look at yourself? Look at yourself and be proud of what the gods have given you. Enjoy your body! You can enjoy it more when you have taken care of it and it pleases your eye.

I also get naked because I know that my body needs to breathe, especially my feet. So I sometimes walk around my house stark naked or scantily clad. Because I live in a secluded area, I have the freedom to be naked in the great outdoors, and I take full advantage of it. At night, particularly rejuvenating is a moonlit walk around my pool area. As every pore of my body is getting a chance to breathe, I am filling up on nature.

Whenever you can get naked without annoying or distracting others, help yourself. (I have found that night swimming, too, is *very* soothing, and water exercises are very, very beneficial: even athletes exercise in a pool, I'm told.)

Have a Ball

Often, when I am away from home for any length of time, I have a medicine ball with me. (Mine is a great weight for me: nine pounds.) When I have a break during a rehearsal or between shows, I work on myself with the medicine ball. For example, for my stomach's sake, I lie on my back with the medicine ball pressed between my knees, and then I go twisting the torso from side to side, knees touching down on the floor each time.

If I have company, we can play catch.

Twiddle Your Fingers

I was fascinated when, in Greece, I noticed people twirling around their fingers what I found out is called a *gambola,* a circle of strung beads with another strand of beads hanging down with a weight on the end, perhaps the size of a quarter. It's on the order of a rosary, only smaller. Its purpose is to kill boredom. But there's more to be had from such an item: fiddling with something like this while waiting in a line, standing or sitting around in conversation, or while watching television can combat stiffness in the hands and relaxes tension. I also work toward nimble fingers by twirling a quarter or a small stone through my fingers (left hand, right hand, left hand, and so on).

Take Care of Your Feet

They say that people carry the weight of the world on their shoulders. Really, it is our feet that bear the load, and yet, the feet are the last thing that many people think about.

Rejuvenate! (It's Never Too Late)

My feet have been through a lot. I ended up with bunions from wearing shoes that were too tight when I was performing with the Dunham company. Tight shoes or not, many people develop bunions because of all the weight that is put on the feet and the wearing of silly shoes. Moreover, we can get corns from the feet sweating up and not being aired out enough.

I did my feet no favor during the years that I wore stiletto heels. Because of my training and vigilance about walking properly, I managed to walk well in stilettos (for a short distance). But it was so tiring, and at times I found myself bending forward a bit to save myself from the foot fatigue. Then, one day I said, "This is ridiculous!"—good-bye, stilettos! High heels, in general, are dangerous: they are bad for the back; the heel can get caught in cracks; and one false move and the ankle can have a mishap. (I love wedgies because in them my whole body seems to be weighted correctly. Flats work well for me, too, unless the shoe has a wide heel.)

When the feet have need, I go to a chiropodist for treatment. Occasionally, I treat my feet to reflexology, and I have a pedicure about once a month. When summertime comes, I cannot wait to get into sandals so my feet can breathe and my toes can wiggle galore.

The health of our feet has an impact on the quality of our walking, and the way we walk affects various parts of our bodies. Need I say more?

Rest

Without rest—no zest. Cooking is restful for me, as is my needlepoint, as is tucking into my rocking chair with a book or just my thoughts.

Do I meditate? Indeed: when I am walking through the woods looking at nature in her glory or watching the animals playing, working, doing their thing. I do not need to sit still in a particular posture to meditate, but I understand how useful such can be.

Real sleep—absolute downtime—is imperative. (Try to get your room as dark as possible.) I listen to the silence or to the crickets when they are out. Sometimes, if I'm working on something new (such as a part in a play) and I need to rest my mind, I find that tuning in to talk radio helps me to think of something else. (I love talk radio: I can get so many things done while I'm being informed.)

Throughout my life, I have generally slept for six or seven

hours a night. If my voice is getting tired, sometimes I force myself to sleep for nine or ten hours. I say "force" because lying in bed for a long time has always seemed to me a waste of time, a waste of life. I figure I'll have enough time to lie about when they put me in my coffin (but I'm not getting into the coffin until I have done the needlepoint).

When I was younger, I never took naps, but with the passage of time, I have found naps to be a great pick-me-up.

Get a Massage

I get a massage about once a month. What a boon to the circulation a massage is. I have come across great masseurs who I wish could travel with me, such as Ken at Shutters in Santa Monica.

If you cannot afford the frequent professional massage, treat yourself to one of those handheld massagers. There's also the loofah massage that you can do while in the bath. Rocking-and-rolling is yet another form of massage. Perhaps, too, you will find that you can afford a professional massage once in a while. If so, buyer beware. As massages have become more and more popular, there are more and more incompetent practitioners on the loose: people who really do not have the training to do deep, heavy massage, to find the muscle strains and excessive tension in every part of the body. If you just want somebody to rub your body, can't you find a friend to do that¿ Or how about your partner¿ Get him or her to oil you down, in which case you never know what it might lead to aside from getting the circulation going.

Avoid Bad Spirits

I pay as much attention to the seen as to the unseen. Sadly, what I see is that there are a lot of negative people in our world. The blatantly wicked ones are really not the major problem: you can't help but be aware of them and will probably naturally avoid or minimize contact with such people. It's those who comport themselves like lambs who present the most danger.

I am always sensing anyone with whom I come in contact. My first impression of a person is never wrong. I can feel in my spirit when someone is not good for me to be around, even if he or she bears a smile or gifts. The hairs on the back of my neck really do stand up. When someone starts with the hugging and kissing, I can feel the vibrations right away—I know if it is real or not. (My back squinches up with the phonies.) Because bad spirits drain and weaken me, I am committed to avoiding them as much as I can. After spending time with so-and-so, do you find yourself cranky, envious, mean-spirited, tired, deflated?

Our ability to pursue positive thinking and outlook (without which positive action is difficult) is greatly affected by the energies of others. So give serious thought to the company you keep. I'd rather keep company with myself than with someone who drains my energy.

Economize

You do not have to spend a lot of money to be fit. If you eat to live, your grocery bill will probably shrink (and so will you).

As for physical exercise, you do not have to belong to a gym or have a personal trainer to get and stay in shape.

Gym workouts are fantastic. Whenever I have an engagement out of town, I always ask to be put up in a hotel that has a gym—and in a room that has a window that opens! Also, I take advantage of the gym at a center near my home.

Not having access to a gym, however, is no excuse not to

exercise. Some feel that joining a gym—spending money—will keep them motivated. Perhaps. Really, only your desire to take care of yourself will motivate you to exercise. No matter how many hundreds of dollars you shell out for a gym membership, if you are not truly committed to your body, you will find one "justifiable" reason after another as to why you cannot go to the gym tomorrow and tomorrow and tomorrow.

Personal trainers are wonderful, too. For the past two years I have worked out, two or three times a week, with the magnificent Radu and with Diane Caruso (for aerobics). A personal trainer can get you doing things that you do not feel like doing and teach you how to do exercises properly. If you cannot afford to work with a trainer regularly, perhaps you can invest in a few sessions to get you on the right track. Or, you can buy an instructional video (like mine!).

When all is said and done, I think that the best exercise is natural exercise: those things that require minimal equipment (if any) and those things you do as part of living your life. As I have already mentioned, walking is one of the best exercises, as is swimming, as is housecleaning, as is playing with children—from board games (for the mind) to ball games (for mind and body).

Here are some more simple exercises that will not cost you anything. As with any exercise, you should be sure that it is right for you before you go for it.

Bounce: Lie on your back with your knees bent and your hands on the floor. Bounce your hips up and down, lightly. This will ease away tension in the middle area of the body. Try to do this about ten times and then repeat three times. (Remember: Repetition is the key to all exercise. The body needs time to realize what's going on so that it can cooperate.)

As you bounce, think about allowing a little more spontaneity into your life.

Jump: With a rope proportionate with your height, jump rope easily, breathing properly all the while and keeping your stomach tight and your shoulders relaxed. I usually jump rope for about fifteen minutes.

Let this exercise give you food for thought on leaping at good opportunities. And if you are going to jump at a chance, you ought to give thought to how you are going to land—as you must do with actual jumping so as not to injure the spine (come down on the balls of your feet and let the knees bend).

Twist: Stand with your feet flat on the floor, knees slightly bent and your fists clenched. Twist easily from side to side without pitching forward. Inhale when you twist; exhale when you return to the center. Left, right, left, right. A sister exercise is to finish the twist by touching the right elbow to the left knee and the left elbow to the right knee. When I do the twist, I usually do about sixteen sets, with two repeats.

Whichever version you opt for, as you twist, consider contorting yourself from time to time and finding a new spin on a routine thing. (Maybe a new way to make chicken? Maybe some really creative gifts instead of what the marketplace pressures you to buy?)

Punch: Stand with your knees slightly bent and your fists clenched. Visualize the air in front of you as a wall and punch it—left, right, left, right. Inhale as one fist goes out; exhale as the other goes out. Try to get in ten or so rapid punches with each arm, and repeat twice.

No, don't think violent thoughts as you do this exercise, but do think about being aggressive for the sake of good. Fight for yourself and the things that you believe in. Go for it when the "it" is a needed or useful thing for you or for people about whom you care. Do not be so quick to retreat when you come upon resistance (from within or from without). Do not always wait for an opening—make one!

Don't Overrate or Underrate Sex

Thanks to Viagra and the like, many older people are feeling pressured to turn up the volume in bed. Sex is exciting (and can be a nice workout), and food helps.

A great sensible meal and the sex connection—wow! All the senses explode. A glass of good wine with a good meal can stimulate the sex desire, at least for me. But the desire can descend when too many glasses are taken in an effort to keep the feeling strong.

The smell of a person also stimulates. The French have said that the true body odor tells you the truth about that loving feeling. At times, I found myself feeling incredibly amorous toward a man only to find out that I was really smitten with his cologne. Once the cologne wore off, and I got a whiff of the real man, I lost interest in bedroom gymnastics.

Neither men nor women should allow themselves to be used sexually. Those who do only cheat themselves. I got to a point (years and years ago) when I got weary of being used as a sex object. (Many men wanted to lay me down, but few wanted to pick me up.) I resented becoming a notch in the belt, especially when I needed a hamburger and not a shot of Scotch. (That I poured on the floor or in a flowerpot many times.) Life is too valuable for you to allow yourself to be used as a sex toy (the soul gets abused and the mind damaged).

When I became what is termed a senior citizen, I began to feel like a real person. I was no longer concerned about having an unnecessary man in my life. I have always depended on my own wits to survive (never really needed a man to pay my bills, so to speak). To have a man for my womanly satisfaction—great. To prove myself a woman by having a man—no.

Sex is good when we are good to ourselves and to each other in every way. Sex can enhance your well-being—good sex, that is (which is not about position or duration, but honesty between two people). I think more good sex can be had without extraordinary measures than people realize. The better your health—body and mind—the better the sex. As I have said, a great meal can bring on a desire for sex: fish, a green salad with a vinegar-and-olive-oil dressing (no onions!), and a baked potato (I prefer sweet, and no butter)—such a meal can be a great aphrodisiac. There is nothing like pure olive oil and fish to heighten all five senses, and they are all connected to the sexual appetite. (Now this is me talking, not a dietitian.)

Take Care of the Planet

The health of the environment we all share has an impact on our well-being. I will not offer a discourse here on global warming and such. You know what is happening. Too many people are bringing too many people into the world . . . the massacre of forest after forest . . . the ever-encroaching cement . . . the ever-mounting garbage dumps because we consume like crazy: food, drink, clothing, toys, cars, plastic bags, foil, cardboard, paper, electronic and mechanical gizmos and gadgets, et cetera, et cetera—and let's not forget energy.

Stop and think about how much garbage you create. Think of ways that you can reduce your waste. Try your utmost to recycle. And, yes, why not plant a tree?

Use well the land around you, no matter how small the area. It saddens me to see empty spaces in New York City and elsewhere: land that could be used for gardens of some kind. It saddens me, too, when buildings are erected on these spaces with no room for even a small garden or a tree or two.

How healthy can we be living on an ailing planet? Remember: everything is connected, and if we care for the planet, the planet will care for us.

Acknowledgments

Special thanks to Al Lowman, Tonya Bolden, B. G. Dilworth, Duva, Daryl Waters, Jaki Harris, Milagros, Carlo Geraci, Art Robbins, Katy Chan, Jane Chan, George Fearon, Peter Fields, Diane Caruso, The Hotel Carlyle, and Aba and Mutzi. And to all those who have shown me unconditional love.